CHICKEN GENIUS

The Art of Toshi Sakamaki's Yakitori Cuisine

BERNARD RADFAR

FOREWORD BY NOBU MATSUHISA
PHOTOGRAPHS BY ARAM RADFAR

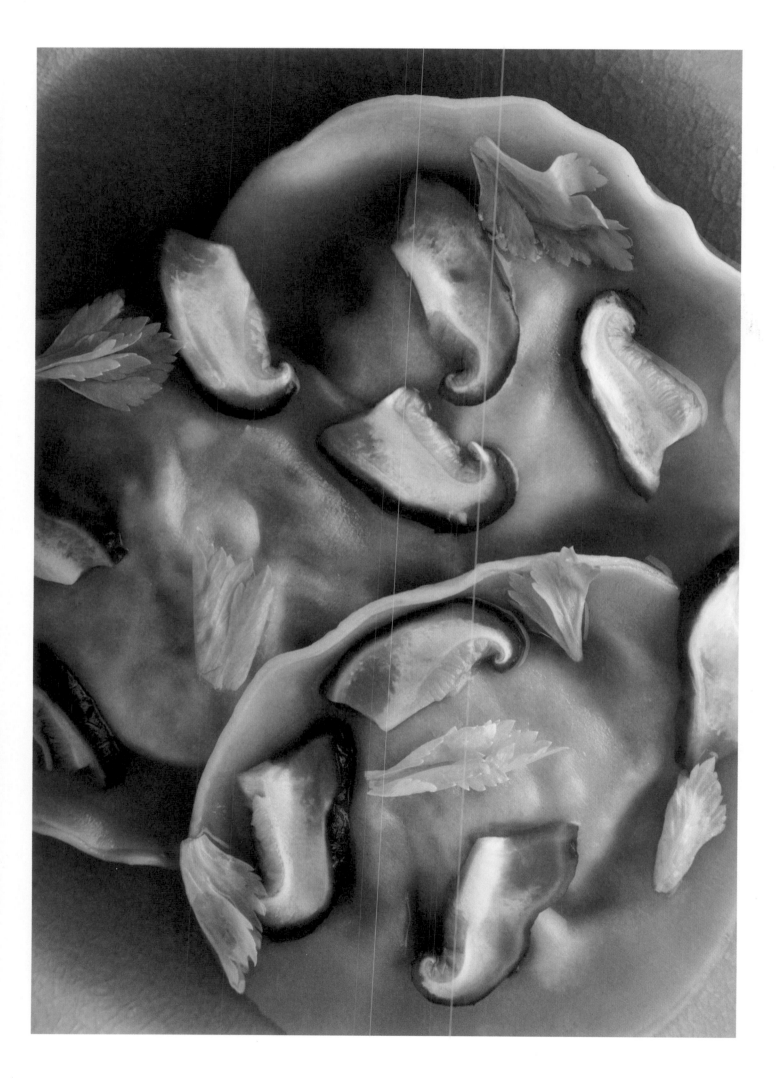

Our cooking depends upon shadows and is inseparable from darkness.

The quality that we call beauty must always grow from the realities of life.

—Jun'ichirō Tanizaki

CHICKEN GENIUS

Photographs by Aram Radfar

The Art of Toshi Sakamaki's Yakitori Cuisine

BERNARD RADFAR

FOREWORD BY NOBU MATSUHISA

Rare Bird ✦ Los Angeles, Calif.

Celebration is for being quiet and composed.

—Shijo Takashima

FOREWORD BY NOBU MATSUHISA

YAKITORI. The word makes me hungry, as I remember the humble places in Japan where chicken is handled with honor and simplicity. Chef Toshimitsu Sakamaki has dedicated himself to our culinary tradition, quietly serving some of the greatest yakitori in the world—right here in Los Angeles.

Like all great chefs, he expands our idea of what can be done with an ingredients handled in the purest manner.

I love to enter Yakitoriya and put my trust in Toshi-san's hands. Not all Westerners understand the nature of this exchange, but for me it is an essential part of what dining implies. A relationship is established over decades or even generations, and in Japan it is an essential fabric of daily life. It defines the culture itself.

Yakitori isn't only about chicken, any more than sushi is only raw fish. And yet it is exactly that. Great care is taken with each selection and cut. A dish is composed much like an artist who faces the canvas. Juxtapose this with most places we encounter, where quality is not the guiding principle, as it ought to be.

This book, therefore, is both an introduction and a celebration of yakitori.

Allow yourself to enter the world of it, as it is a rewarding one. There's elegance in it, warming yourself by the fire, in expectation of the next skewer. Being with loved ones, sharing a bottle of sake, and drinking the purest of broths. Great food such as this has the power to transform us.

I hope this book gives readers the experience of being at Toshi-san's counter, and helps spread awareness of the importance in feeding and eating well. We all need nourishment and beauty. It is after all a journey we are all on, and how we eat and cook and serve seems to me to be an issue of ultimate importance.

20 BILLION CHICKENS

THERE IS NOTHING EXOTIC about chicken, at least not anymore.
It is estimated that this most populous bird on the planet num-
bers around twenty billion, with roughly nine billion slaugh-
tered annually in the USA alone. It was the first descendant of
the dinosaurs to be domesticated, and the only livestock the
slaves here were allowed to own. Apparently, people love or
need them more than we are aware. And, therefore, much more
great yakitori needs to be prepared.

INTRODUCTION BY TOSHIMITSU SAKAMAKI

YAKITORI IS MY WAY, you could say. Through chicken and the art of yakitori, I express myself and what I know. I came to it because the first time I had it prepared well, I was shocked by how delicious it was. In my opinion, this is the best way of preparing a chicken.

Every morning I need to return to the market to get chicken. The life of this animal is a gift from nature. I have to honor that life in what I do. We take life to have life. So it is important to me not to waste any of the chicken. To present it in all its beauty.

Chickens don't care about religion and politics. We make food because of pleasure. Everyone but vegetarians can eat chicken, but we often fail to honor the animal and nature in a special way. I suspect that as the population of the world increases, chicken will prove to be an even more important food source. Yakitori is evolving as well, both in Japan and here. I don't worry about changes to the tradition, but what we make should taste good. I still think the traditional style is the best, but I am open to other ways. That is why I wish to share what I know in my kitchen, what I do every day.

I came to yakitori through sushi, having first worked at a small fish market in Japan. When I came to Los Angeles, I worked at a sushi restaurant. But I was shocked by the quality of the seafood back then. I knew I didn't want to be a sushi man here, so I began looking for another field. Eventually I got a job at a yakitori place, through which I learned a great deal of what I know. The first time I grilled something for myself, I knew this could be what I would do. I had never known chicken could be so special. Through the work, I came to love yakitori. It became so much of my life. That is what I wish this book will share with others.

A HISTORY OF YAK

It takes many centuries for a tradition to take root. This is difficult for some in the New World to accept. In Japan, the inn you stay at might go back thirty generations in the same family. The same is probably the case with the pickle vendor in Kyoto; nothing has changed in his recipe, nor in his competitor's. The same can't be said for yakitori, a relative newcomer, though aspects of the cuisine relate to hunting in samurai times. To my knowledge, a comprehensive history of yakitori has yet to be written. As far back as the 17th century, there have been Japanese debates and recipes concerning the grilling of birds. Given that Japanese society has been mostly xenophobic and pescatarian, the adoption of chicken as a regular part of the diet wasn't going to occur overnight. Only with European influence did chicken become the bird of choice, replacing duck, quail, sparrow, and other hunted varieties. More often than not, chickens were raised inland, a few days from fresh seafood. Even if the Japanese had a taste for poultry, an economy needed to develop. Records exist about the expansion of poultry farms from prefecture to prefecture during the past three centuries. Initially, chicken was considered a great delicacy, as it was not widely available. And, if you can imagine, it was more expensive than beef. After World War II, countless drinking establishments became popular, as people sought quick, tasty foods and drink on their way home from work. The resemblance of yakitori stands to kebab stands across the Middle East is uncanny, but exactly why they look alike, we may never know for certain. Could it be (and this is my guess) that one lone traveler to Isfahan or Beirut returned home with a great idea? Some say that the first yakitori stand was built outside a popular Kyoto temple, giving it a holy heritage, for those who require that. Eventually, certain neighborhoods became renowned for their yakitori restaurants. As with anything in Japan, the concept of grilled chicken was refined gradually so that today some of the finest establishments in every city are yakitori restaurants. Still, whereas kaiseki (or even sushi) is serious and formal, yakitori is about drinking and having a good time. I will go so far as to say that being near a fire should do that to us: it should make us laugh. It always has.

YAKITORIYA: A PERSPECTIVE BY BERNARD RADFAR

Good food is the foundation of genuine happiness. —Auguste Escoffier

BEAUTY IS QUIET.

It hints at truths.

Eventually we realize that little else matters.

Descending from the skies, we find a neighborhood. Life's basics occur: loving, walking, a face in a window. This becomes our cherished memories: trees planted and children returning from school freer.

Even here, in a city often detested, a city dismissed as in no way a city (as if any metropolis is or isn't). Yet many who've journeyed the globe find in Los Angeles a hidden charm for which they've been hungering, a harmony with place and time.

For me it involves a restaurant: Yakitoriya.

In my journey, home to Los Angeles, I return again and again to Yakitoriya, and my place at the "Chicken Grilling Establishment." I dare call this hideaway one of the Seven Wonders of the World, a haven of civility far removed from the haste and pressure that squeezes life. Something transcendent occurs at Yakitoriya, something elemental.

And I hate chicken.

Art is made of what surrounds us on a daily basis. Sound is everywhere, but composers use it to layer our lives with meaning. Words are all over, but writers plumb their depths to reveal realities anew. Who knew that the same could be done with a chicken and some charcoal?

Not I, until coming to know Toshi, Yakitoriya's founder.

Many of us have been fortunate to experience what the great Japanese masters communicate through sushi. Practically overnight, they've transformed the world's palette. It turns out that serving raw fish on white rice can evoke the heavens. The sushi masters have made us ravenous for the raw and minimal. Through the plate they have interpreted the sea and revealed a great culture. That same impulse and tradition applied to the ubiquitous chicken has gone largely unnoticed outside of Japan. Here, we eat chicken nonstop, as a source of protein that we hardly honor. Yet on the streets and in six-seat shacks since the last big war, Japan's culinary philosophers have been pondering and fiddling with chicken. Just as most cans of tuna have little to do with a delicate cut of toro, so our chicken has little to do with the Japanese inventions.

So much is neglected, after all.

How many of us think to divide a chicken thigh into sections for various purposes? Or make three (let alone any) distinct delicacies from a chicken heart. Toshi does. He has reasons. You needn't know them, but your senses will know them, should you be lucky enough to try his cooking, or to read his chapter on butchering in this book.

Many people don't get it when I tell them yakitori is the new sushi—or when I suggest that raw chicken might be better than raw fish. Yet this prejudiced lot loves steak tartare and oysters. And those among them who have dared try toriwasa, a dish made with raw chicken and egg, begin to change their minds.

We are always assuming, even when we know that we are perpetually misinformed.

There is little glory and great humbleness in saying that you serve exclusively chicken.

It is precisely for this reason that I dare to shine a flashlight on a quiet world that I hope, with all my being, will remain so—and on this genius: Toshi.

Toshi has turned some of us into addicts, even those never before addicted to anything. We can't stray far from his creations. More than once, I have dashed over to Yakitoriya after an international flight.

Yakitori has become my priority.

Toshi didn't believe it when I said I would be relocating for only one reason: to be in walking distance from him. Were there an apartment over the restaurant, I would have rented it. But I got close enough. I walk—but in my imagination, I float through sake-flooded alleys—to Yakitoriya.

Admittedly, I am a glutton, eager for tastes and experiences, refined and honed. Yakitoriya makes the worst of days the best, and adds meaning to life. For isn't this what pleasure craves to be? What every meal and conversation ought at least to promise?

I live in fictions, as a novelist. And yet Yakitoriya is ever so real. It is real, and yet it suggests another time and another way of life.

So should this book. It is about a way of cooking, but also about a place and a way of living.

About Los Angeles and Sawtelle Japantown

Los Angeles isn't the only city in the world with conges-tion, freeways, and two-faced people, but it gets a bad rap for it. On the flip side, the city is full of creative people and refugees from around the world. With them comes a vast range of immigrant foods that help make life more enjoyable. Los Angeles is home to the largest Japanese population in the United States, so I'm never too far from a grocer with sashimi. Yakitoriya sits in Japantown, a recently renamed corner of West Los Angeles, beside the roar of the 405. It's a humble neighborhood whose history relates to Japanese internment during World War II, and now it is undergoing transformation into an Asian culi-nary mecca that is no longer exclusively Japanese. Modest homes and plant nurseries on quiet streets are being torn down to make way for the parachute kids of overpopu-lated countries. And traffic comes to a halt at lunch and again at night, as flocks of diners arrive, looking for some of the country's best noodles.

Many of you will never make it to the restaurant, but find-ing or creating something that serves you in a similar manner would be a noble pursuit. Anything of value should have that effect on us: it should teach us and remind us of how to live.

Yakitoriya may not seem like much upon entrance. Chick-en restaurants rarely do. No lighting designers, outside inves-tors, or marketing consultants were brought in to hype the chef's concept. Nothing is advertised. The food is what com-municates.

In the back is a kitchen so clean that it might be a neatnik's home kitchen. In that secret world, for over twenty years, Toshi has overseen each and every skewer as a work of art. He has arranged and treated dishes with the same attention as a sushi master who knows how many grains of rice best hold a certain slice of fish.

There are no plaques on the walls from the institutions that gave themselves the right to judge. A drawing of a chicken in the window serves as the only invitation.

And still, so many people don't understand what is hap-pening. They complain because Toshi won't serve their skewers all at once. Of course he could, and turn more tables. But that's not what interests him. You must wait your turn because a large staff would mean less control. The sequence of the skewers be-comes part of the ritual. The regulars know to laugh and drink when things get busy. Rushing isn't the point. It never is.

I suggest that you arrive alone or with someone whom you trust will not distract you. Plop down on one of the modest stools at the counter, and behold the musician at work by the fire. I sug-gest, even insist, that you be quiet for a moment at least. Absorb the experience so that it will infect the rest of your life.

If you're a group, grab a table. The counter isn't for that. You may have to drink and wait for a menu.

Waiting is part of the music.

Seeing a raw skewer in Toshi's hands, you'll get hungrier. It's a tease.

He will place it on the fire, but not just any fire, a fire of wood carefully dried into charcoal in traditional kilns, the way it has been done for centuries. The charcoal suits the skewer.

Toshi takes scissors and snips away any charred bits. De-pending on the temperature, he might relocate your skewer to another side of the grill. And he'll spin the meat to guarantee that both sides are even, perfectly juicy. He'll cook the fattiest piece in the center, because that's where the grill is hottest.

You get hungrier, watching.

And finally, he will place the warm skewer in front of you, on a ceramic platter.

And you can leave the broken world behind.

Simple is not Simple: Toward a Philosophy of Yakitori
Or Life Outside Chicken, Even

For me this is a bond, what a restaurant should be, something like friendship, based on an honor that flows both ways. Rare individuals like Toshi embody such friendship in all they do.

Honor is a virtue that is worth our attention as individuals and as a culture. So much that is essential to society is considered passé, these days. To serve someone food is to be entrusted with the provision of nourishment, of beauty, of a moment together.

Nowhere do I experience this more than at Toshi's counter. It is why I go night after night.

Through Toshi's chicken, I understand and like the world.

Once I realized how important this was to me, I got up the nerve to ask Toshi what he thought about a book on his cooking.

He seemed surprised. Again, he does his work without a concern for awards or reviews.

"But my food is so simple," he said.

It was the one answer I hadn't expected. Certainly he must know how special he is. "Well, is preparing sushi simple?" I asked.

There was a long pause as Toshi hurried around the kitchen, worried about a busy night ahead. Perhaps it was his way of contemplating the subject of simplicity. "Yes, sushi is simple," he said.

The conversation ended there. He had work to get done.

Connoisseurs certainly recognize that sushi isn't simple. And yet, what does it require? A knife, rice, and nori, a slice of some creature from the sea. Little else.

Forget what most people consider sushi (torpedo rolls, California rolls, inside-out pancake rolls with crunchy fried bits). The masters of the form undertake a lifetime's focus to hand you an astounding cut of fish. They don't sleep at night so they can make it closer to their ideal.

Like the sushi masters, Toshi also has a different understanding of what it means to be simple.

Maybe it is something so profound that it can't be taught. Maybe it can be defined as a dedication to something basic. Either way, few of us can submit to the discipline required. For Einstein and Erdös, math and physics were simple. For Vermeer, the light.

Vision can be simple. But good luck seeing it.

Weeks later, I stand beside Toshi as he selects from various mounds of offal to skewer. "You know," I say, "this is not simple at all. Do you see that?"

"Simple," he repeats. A long pause.

I want to laugh. He is a kind man, never terse. He seems to be thinking about how to tell me.

He lays a skewer on a tray. "It is simple. But it is deep."

That was the moment when I knew that we would produce this book. He had allowed me, as he skewered chicken hearts, to glimpse his world. I was grateful for his respect.

While we developed a certain quiet friendship and trust in the creation of this book, it always embarrassed Toshi, I think, to feel my attention on his workings. My awe only grew as I watched him: That he cared so much about his skewers! That he did so much, in the quiet of his kitchen! I came to see him as Atlas, holding up the dining world.

When I told him the title, Toshi cringed.

"Don't worry, it is my title," I said. "It is what I think of you. In no way do you have to feel responsible."

Time and again, I had to release him that way. "I write the book in homage to you," I'd say. "No description should distract from the person you are, day in and day out."

Toshi doesn't claim to have answers. He does his thing.

He does it in spite of a world where chicken is misunderstood.

An industry exists to make sure you eat horrible chicken. Restaurants will serve it to you at exorbitant prices.

They trick us into eating lots of things you could've prepared or grown far better at home.

I hope we stop. Ask what around is dedicated to our betterment and pleasure.

There is beauty to discover and make, alas.

Simply, deeply.

But what is the use in my pouring out my whole intellect on this subject? I have shown the Western New York Poultry Society that they have taken to their bosom a party who is not a spring chicken by any means, but a man who knows all about poultry, and is just as high up in the most efficient methods of raising it as the president of the institution himself. I thank these gentlemen for the honorary membership they have conferred upon me, and shall stand at all times ready and willing to testify my good feeling and my official zeal by deeds as well as by this hastily penned advice and information. Whenever they are ready to go to raising poultry, let them call for me any evening after eleven o'clock.

—MARK TWAIN

EQUIP-
MENT

Outside of Japan, yakitori has suffered because any number of restaurants add it the menu without giving special care to the chicken. People are led to assume that yakitori simply means any meat cooked on a bamboo skewer at an Asian restaurant. This is partially because Izakayas—a uniquely Japanese food and drink establishment—offer wide menus, including yakitori and sushi. People in Japan know they're probably not getting the best of either although the quality can still be staggeringly high. People who want the best yakitori know to go to a yakitori restaurant. They may serve non-chicken items, the way a sushi restaurant might serve more than fish. But the moment the emphasis is no longer on the chicken, customers know they're not in the hands of someone representing the yakitori tradition.

The Grill

Yes, for yakitori, you'll need one. But any will do, however tiny. A hole in the ground would even suffice. As for the tradition, it is about a narrow grill of some kind that can accommodate skewers. Unlike in the Middle East, the skewers are short, probably because that way you can control the temperature better. For those of you wanting a piece of yakitori art, order a clay Konro grill from Japanese Knife Imports. Or make a grill of your own, out of fire bricks, for example. Toshi uses a stainless steel restaurant grade yakitori grill. Cleaning the pit regularly is mandatory, it adds to the purity of the taste.

Binchō-tan—White Charcoal

You can judge a book by its cover. Binchō, too. Each piece has a way of speaking. The goal with this charcoal made of Ubame oak mirrors the essence of Japanese culinary philosophy: avoid getting in the way of the ingredient. It is known to be the charcoal that imparts the least flavor to what's grilled, while burning evenly. That's probably due to the purity of the sticks, at 97 percent carbon. The flame is relatively small but the heat is intense. Binchō are prized for being smokeless and lasting for several hours.

If on a budget, you can try other woods, or mix them, while leaving the binchō on top, given the relative expense of grilling with bincho. My experience is that nothing tastes like food cooked on bincho. As an experiment, I've grilled identical mackerel on gas and bincho and could hardly believe it was the same fish. However, a debate rages amongst yakitori chefs, a few arguing that the consistency of gas flames trumps the virtues of bincho.

Bincho absorbs the food you grill, so chefs usually don't mix meats. It is why Toshi doesn't expand his menu, concerned about how other drippings would affect the taste of his chicken. Unless you've a grill large enough to guarantee this, stick to one type of meat on your charcoal. Like so much in Japan, there are grades of bincho. How evenly they heat, depending on their manufacturing methods, affects the price. It can easily take as many as thirty years for an Ubame oak tree to become suitable for being converted to charcoal. Lesser grades of charcoals from other countries tend to crack, for example. Those made in Kishu are still often dried in kilns by hand. Forests are managed so that there will be bincho in the future, unlike in some countries. The result is a product incomparable to any other charcoal I've ever tried.

The Knife

Butchers and chefs have debated this one ad infinitum. Toshi uses this small tool you see pictured in this book for almost everything. It allows him the versatility to butcher while not being too heavy to maneuver. That means less wear and tear on his body. Regular sharpening is key, and learning to use a block or maintain your knives with someone who does will only add to your pleasure in the kitchen. The knife does affect the flavor and texture of the food. Sloppy cuts and tears are both visible and noticed, which is why sushi chefs requested that the great samurai knife-makers craft their precious tools.

Bamboo Skewers

You'll need many of these. Luckily, they are widely available at Asian markets. Every yakitori place I've been to uses them.

Fan

Some might consider this unnecessary, but yakitori chefs always seem to have one nearby, for tending the fire. Or else they blow on the flame. And keep themselves cool, of course.

We ought to find ways to learn from traditions that honor. How rare that is. Like my composer friend Simon Shaheen says, the exchange can lead to fusion or confusion. For example, Toshi's butchering technique is something to behold. Every motion in the process is orchestrated, none of the creature gets wasted. He works neatly and patiently. Anyone who appreciates design and proportion in anything will share my sentiment. For artistry and craftsmanship have a way of righting the world for a moment. And it is for this reason that certain traditions mean more than any innovation. Before they can make a proper hummus, for example, they're already selling us fifty variations. Perhaps the notion that every man's for himself can't be the way to build a vital culture. One person's whim might not hold up against centuries of composition and contemplation.

INGRE-
DIENTS

The Chicken

Like pretty much anything you plan to cook, the closer to the source the better. The first time I accompanied Toshi in the kitchen, I was surprised that the flesh was still warm and completely odorless. Chicken is a whole lot like seafood that way. If fresh, the meat should resemble a gleaming piece of yellowtail sashimi. Few of you raise your own, but finding a trusted supplier, whether at a farmer's market or butcher, is essential to making outstanding yakitori. Surprisingly, Toshi feels some supermarket free-range chicken is actually rather fresh and usable. Chickens tend not to sit around as long as some other meats, he explains. Yet, it is proving increasingly difficult to find chickens that have been traditionally raised: allowed to roam and fed the best grains. Though industrial chicken is inexpensive and readily available, often it is lacking the full range of flavor of a chicken from a farm.

Miso

A fermented seasoning paste usually made from soybeans, salt, and Aspergillus oryzae (or Koji). Most outside of Japan simply think of miso as a soup. However, there are many variations and colors of miso, covering the full range of the flavor profiles. Few meals in Japan don't include it in one form or another. For yakitori, it is used as a marinade, sweetening certain pieces. The sauce can be used as a counterpoint to the saltiness and simplicity of the rest of the skewers.

Shoyu—Soy Sauce

Mysterious, the inexpensive bottle we all take for granted is the product of centuries of development. Through it we can learn much about the history of the world. Because of science and international trade, it no longer only defines a core ingredient in Asian cooking, having morphed into various sauces, including the Worcestershire (so prominent in Southern barbecue, not by coincidence).

Approximately 400 years ago, miso and shoyu developed into distinct foods. Through cookbooks and trade routes, the spread of shoyu reached nearly every professional and home kitchen throughout Japan. The size of the production plants during the isolationist Edo period were only outnumbered by temples, indicating its importance to the island's inhabitants. Fermented soy sauce that was the norm for all those centuries became nearly replaced by unfermented soy sauce made in modern factories. Acids were used instead of enzymes during the Industrial Era. Western research and techniques were incorporated to reduce the cost of production. It takes far less time to make this way. Preservative additives in modern shoyu significantly altered the taste once again.

My pantry and refrigerator are filled with various kinds of shoyu. For Toshi's Yakitori Sauce, for example, an industrial grade suits the purpose. Every attempt has been made to replicate the texture and nuance of the traditional shoyu. And by the time you grill it, you probably don't need to use a more expensive product. But for a delicate sauce or to dip in, I always turn to something more artisan. Each is different, but how they are can't be put into words. Like all ingredients, one has to learn to use them to suit your palate. It is like coffee or wine or sake. A universe of flavors onto itself, with master craftsmen subtly manipulating the process to bring out distinctive aspects.

Five General Types of Shoyu:

Koikuchi—*Industrial, dark soy sauce made by companies such as Kikkoman.*

Usukuchi—*A lighter colored sauce popular in the Kansai region. It has a higher salt content but doesn't alter the color of foods as much.*

Tamari—*popular with sushi and in teriyaki, and from the area around Nagoya. There is only a hint of alcohol in the product.*

Saishikomo—*From Yamaguchi, this is a much lighter shoyu, with a sweeter but less salty flavor. Often used with eel and for dipping.*

Shiro—*the Japanese word for white, these shoyu are used when you do not want any change in appearance to your food. They have various flavors, however.*

The Japanese government grades each of these, Special (tokkyuu), First (ikkyuu), and Standard Grade (hyoujun). The Japanese Soy Sauce Association adds two higher grades to the Special Grade: Upper Select (tokusen) and Ultra-Extra Select (choutokusen). To read more about the history and grading of soy sauce, I highly recommend The History of Soy Sauce, Shoyu, and Tamari by William Shurtleff and Akiko Aoyagi.

Mustard—Karashi

The verdict isn't out on whether this should be on every yakitori plate. Some places shun it. Yakitoriya certainly doesn't: it ought to be used sparingly; however, given that it should highlight rather than overpower the chicken's flavors. Toshi uses the powdered form to make his paste.

Ponzu

From "Pons," the Dutch word for citrus juice, because of the early contact through maritime trading. While yuzukoshō is made from yuzu (a Japanese citrus) peels, Ponzu begins with the citrus juice and shoyu. Variations on the sauce exist, but most also include some combination of mirin (a cooking wine), vinegar, fish flakes, sugar, and salt. It is a widely used in much of Japanese cooking and is available commercially, though you can easily make your own.

Sancho Pepper

Whole or ground, these citrusy seedpods of the Japanese prickly ash taste like no other pepper. Used on specific skewers (meatball and hearts, for example), a dash goes a long way. Too much and you'll be numb in fact.

Shichimi Togarashi—Seven Chili Pepper Blend

A blend of seven chili peppers, these are used in a variety of dishes. In yakitori, regulars keep a bit on the serving plate to add spiciness and texture to certain skewers. I purchase mine at the tiny Gion Hararyoukaku in Kyoto, where they've been on offer since no earlier than 1704.

Wasabi

That powdery green mound on your sushi plate has its origin in an indigenous horseradish, Wasabia Japonica, that thrives in the flowing streams of Japan. Some are now grown hydroponically, with great results. There are eight general cultivars of wasabi, with different levels of heat. Fresh wasabi rhizomes can be found at some Japanese suppliers abroad, and are far more expensive than the dried powder mix that usually has little or no wasabi in it. The paler the fresh wasabi rhizome, the better. The sweetness quickly disappears after picking as they dry out, so use it within the week. There are tubes of wasabi pastes available that contain actual wasabi and are a far better substitute to the powder.

Yuzukosho

A real treat, this fermented condiment from the southern island of Kyushu consists of Yuzu (a Japanese citrus) peels, spicy chili peppers, and salt. It is widely available in jars and tubes at Japanese markets. Or you can make your own. There are two general types of yuzukoshō: red and green. Toshi uses the latter on skewers such as the duck breast, given its sharper, more citrusy flavor. The peppers used to make yuzukoshō are usually bird's eye chilies.

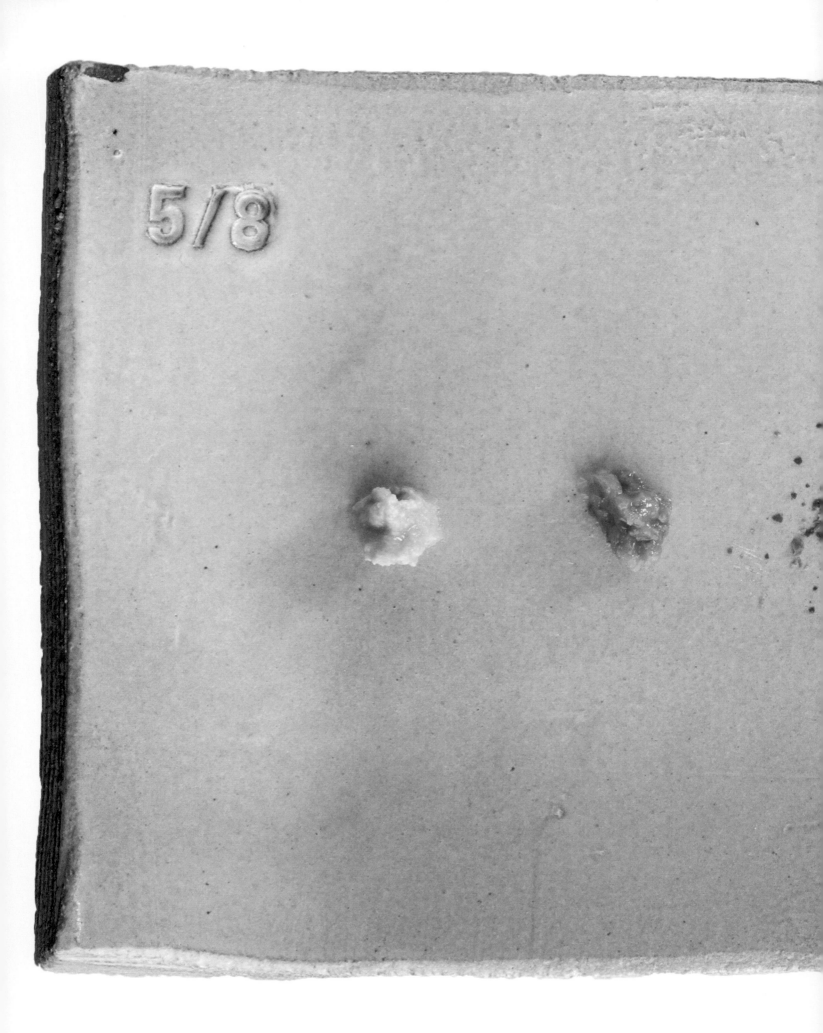

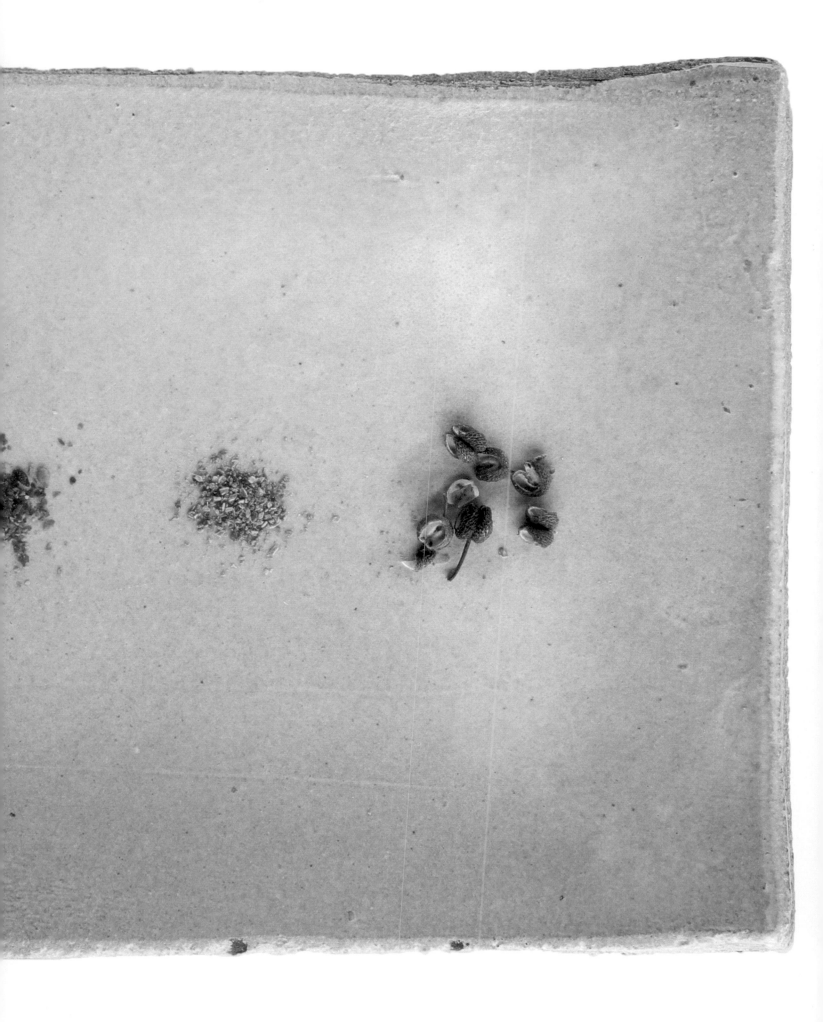

APPE-
TIZERS

Giblet Stew

Soborro Rice

Deep Fried Gizzard

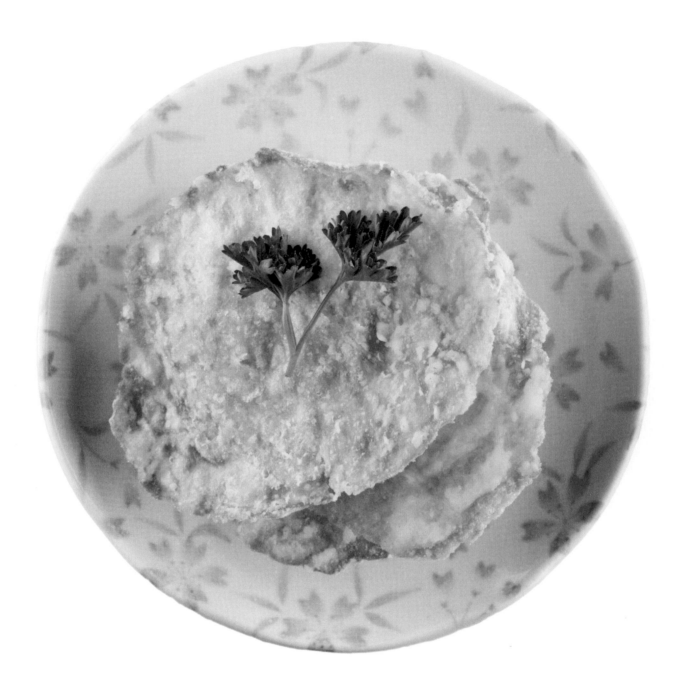

Chicken Finger Cutlet Filet

Premature Egg Yolk

My hope is that this cookbook represents what's served at Yakitoriya, presented as is. To inspire you to cook more, as we learn about the serene world of Toshi's kitchen. I have chosen to lean on the side of the minimal with my directives. Recipes have a way of hanging us up, being intimidating so that we leave our feeding to the experts. There isn't one way to do or cook something any more than there is one way to walk. Whether a quarter or full teaspoon of pepper is added to a dish is usually debatable or individual. Five tablespoons or none might work best, even if it goes against convention. In fact, it ought to, given the status quo. My goal herein: to celebrate the simplest of cuisines by writing about it in a way that reflects its quality. The kitchen, a lab most every home comes with, ought to be a place to play and find solace. We can all learn greatly from the kind of discipline, devotion and excellence that infuses Toshi's life.

SKEW-ERS

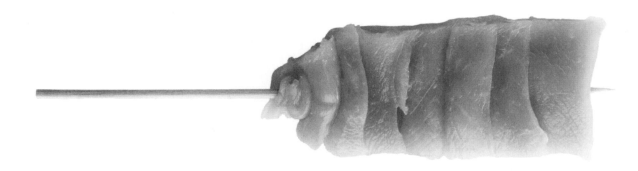

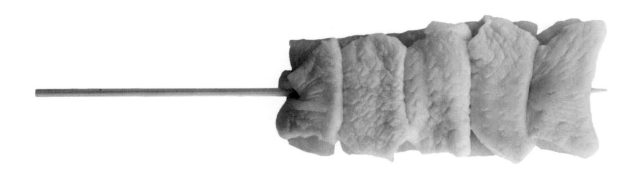

Breast (uncooked)—Breast with Skin (uncooked)—Breast with Wasabi (cooked)

Ankle (uncooked)—Ankle (cooked)—Soft Bone (uncooked)—Tail (uncooked)—Chest Bone (cooked)

Duck Stick (cooked)—Duck Stick (uncooked)

Gizzard (uncooked)—Gizzard (cooked)

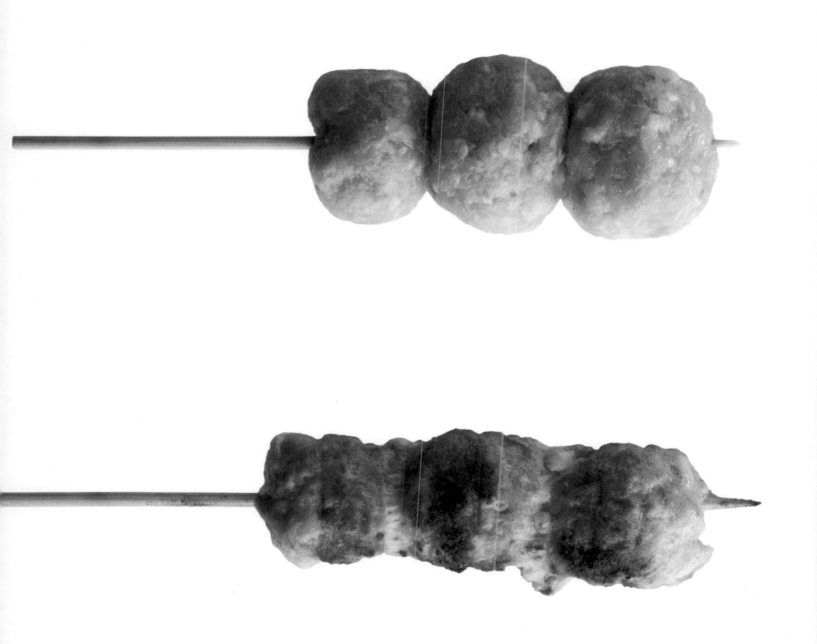

Special Special Heart (cooked)—Special Special Heart (uncooked)—Whole Heart (cooked)—Whole Heart (uncooked)

Special Heart (uncooked)—Special Heart (cooked)—Heart (uncooked)—Heart (cooked)   5 9

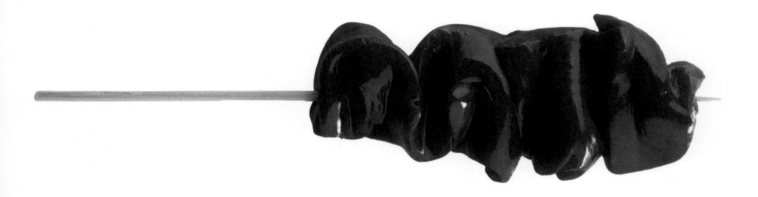

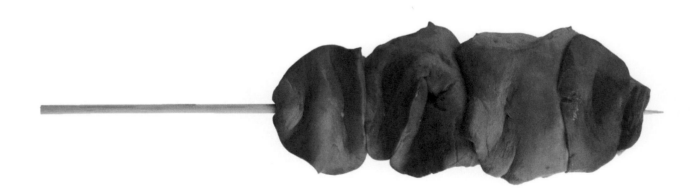

White Liver (cooked)—Liver (uncooked)—White Liver (uncooked)

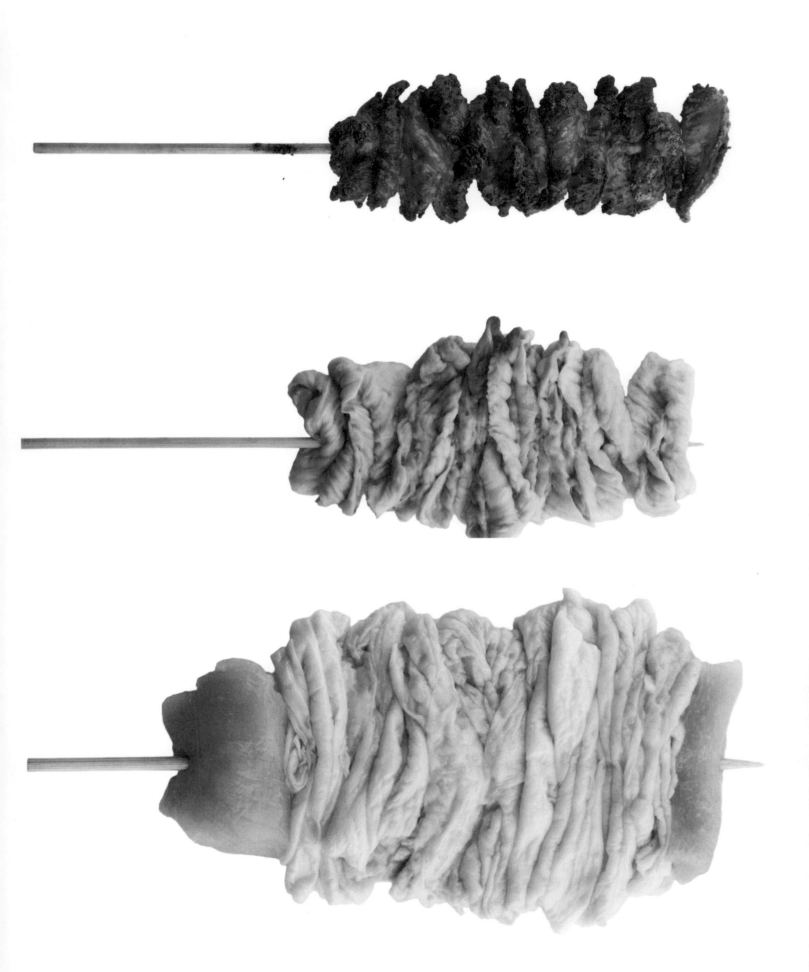

Wing Skin (cooked)—Wing Skin (uncooked)—Skin (uncooked)

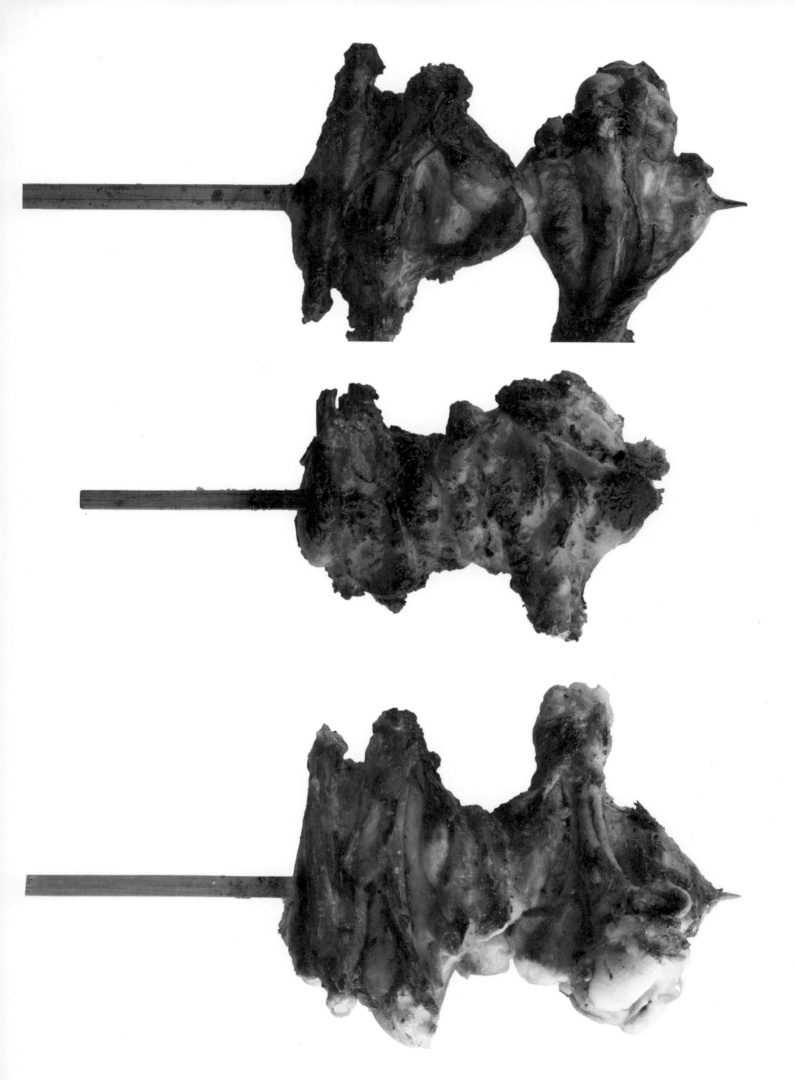

Spicy Wing (cooked)—Miso Wing (cooked)—Wing (cooked)

Okra (uncooked)—Okra (cooked)—Asparagus (uncooked)

Green Onion (uncooked)—Green Onion (cooked)—Shishito (uncooked)

Shitake (uncooked)—Shitake (cooked)

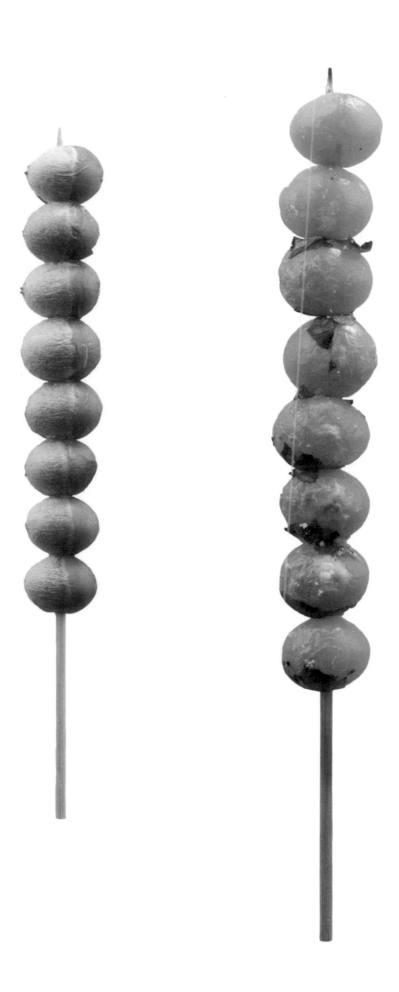

Turnip (uncooked)—Turnip (cooked)—Zucchini (cooked)

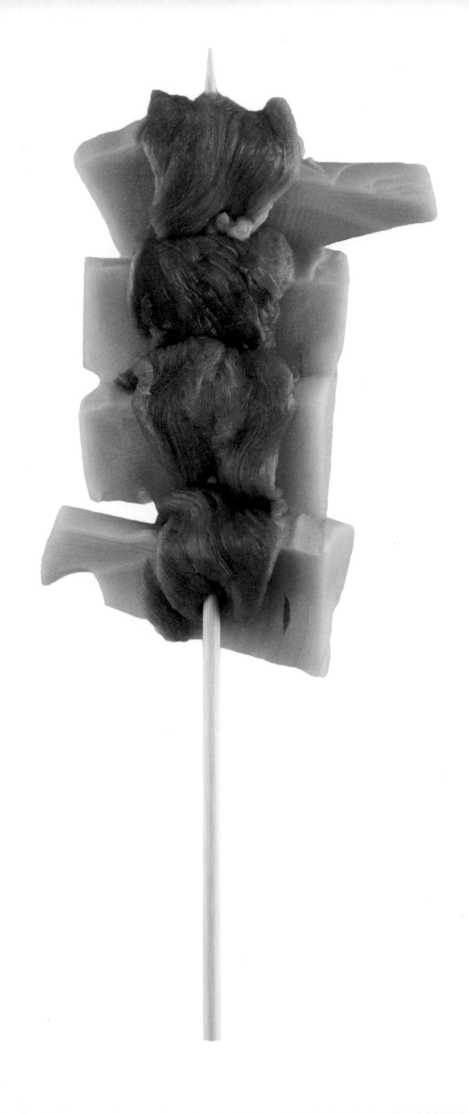

Bamboo Shoot (uncooked)

SKEW-
ERING

It has been said of Japanese food that it is to be looked at rather than eaten. I would go further and say that it is to be meditated upon. Tanazaki, In Praise of Shadows. Putting ingredients on a stick isn't enough, in whatever order you happen to reach for them. That's what's usually done, if you think about it. Not here. Each skewer is composed, from conception. Handled and cut in a manner so that by the time you eat it, there might be transcendence. All your senses, including your eyes, can appreciate to the fullest each aspect of the final product.

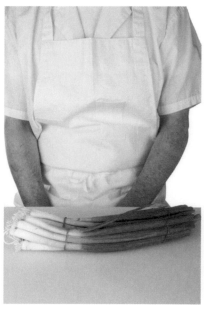

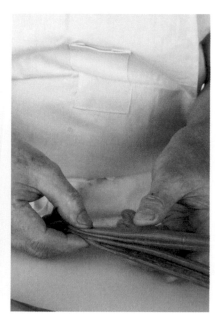

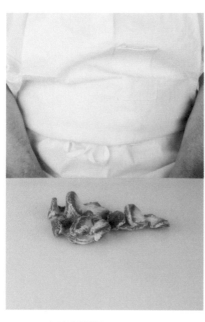

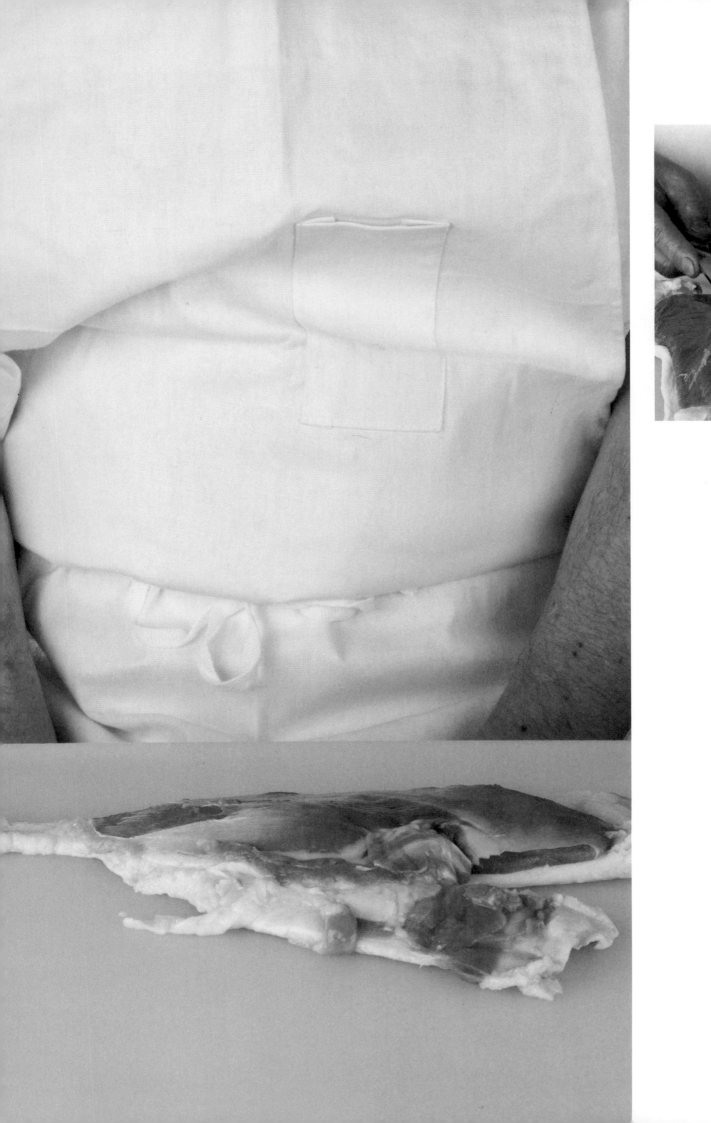

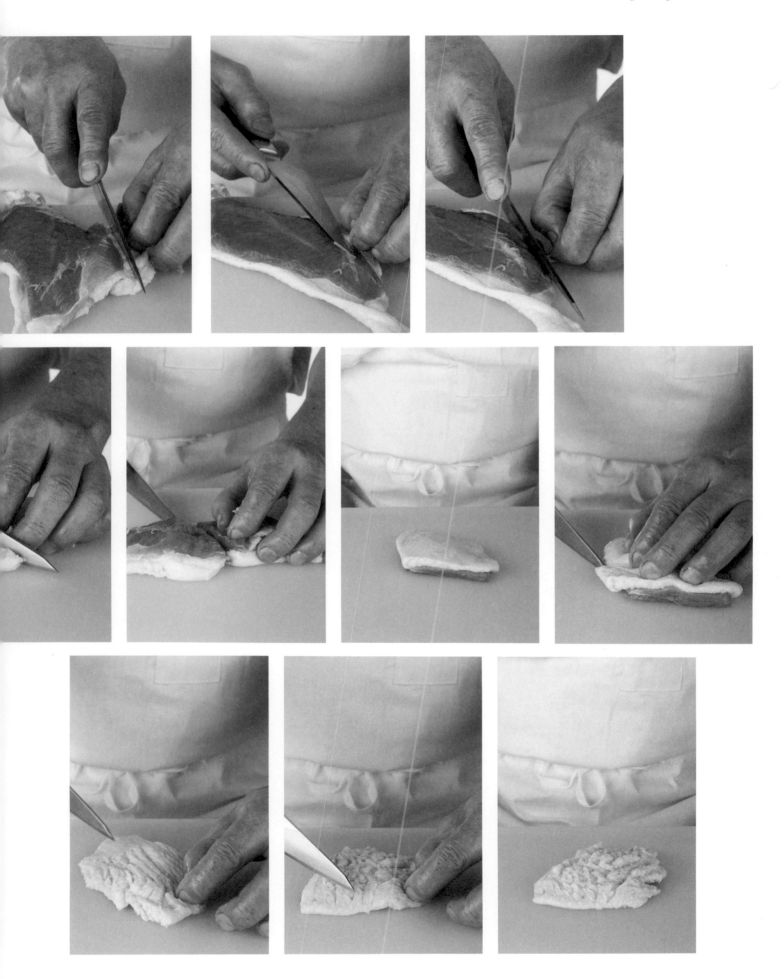

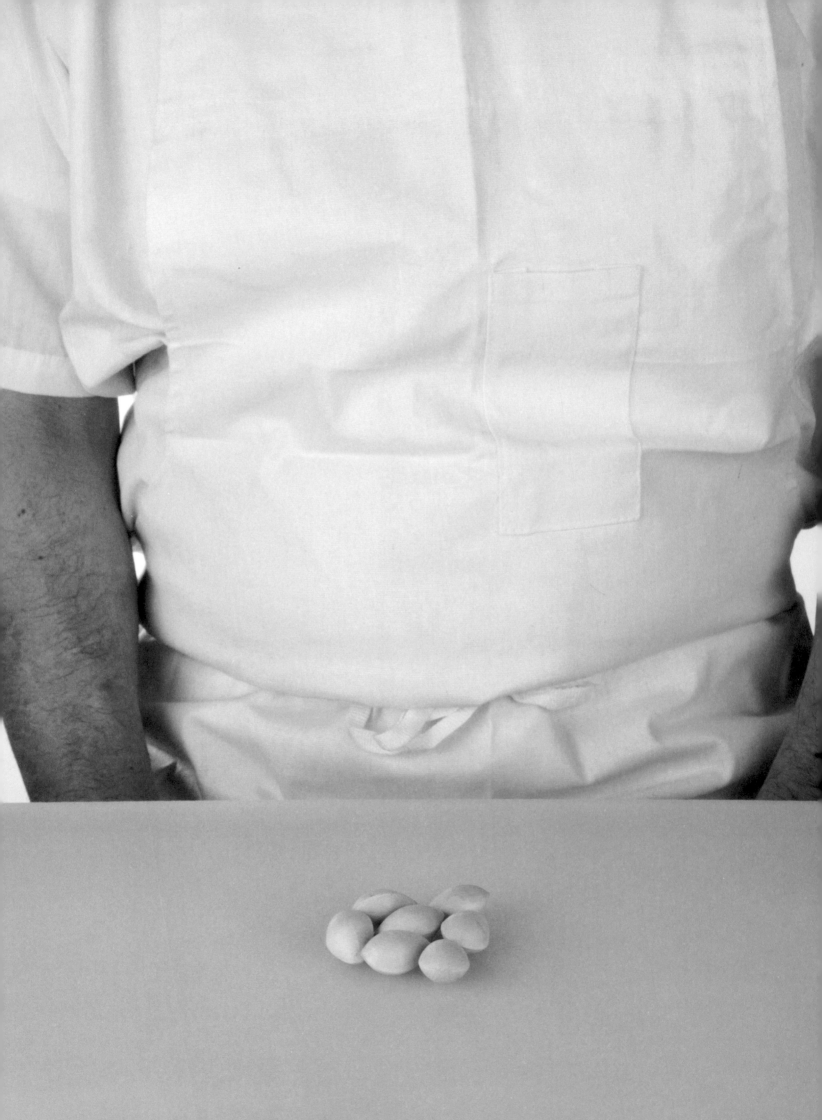

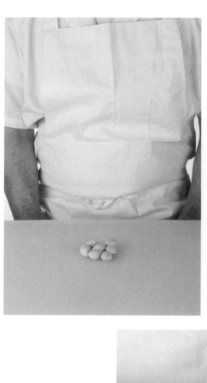
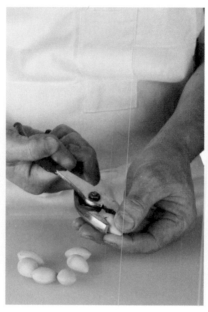
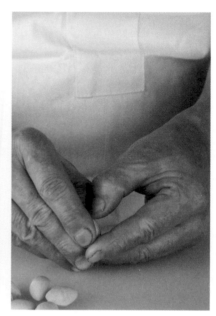

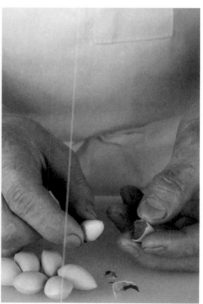

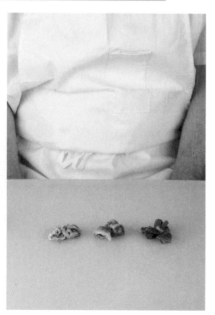

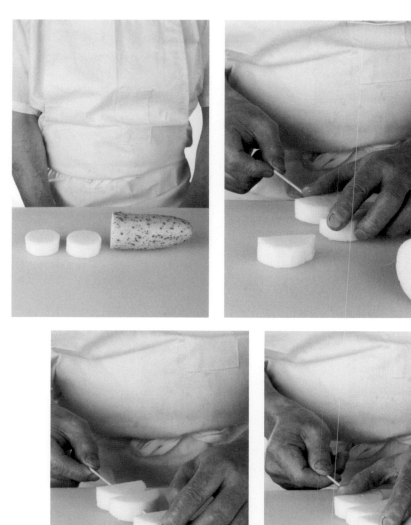

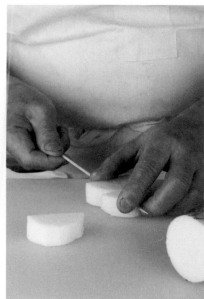

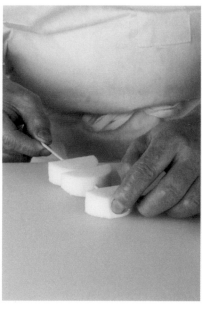

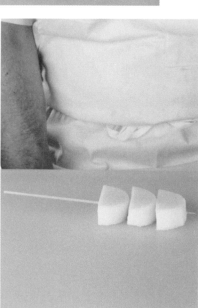

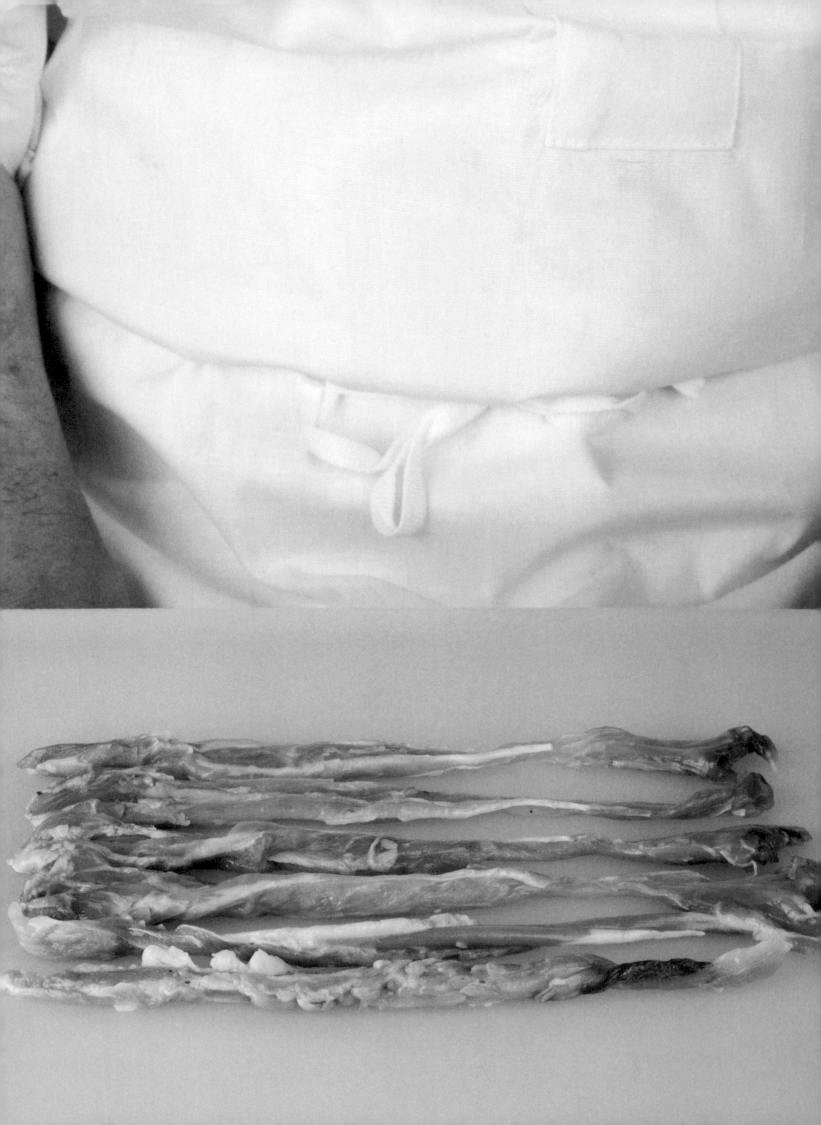

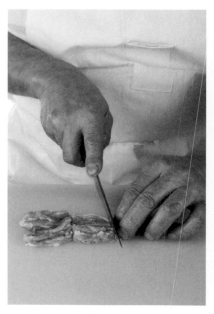

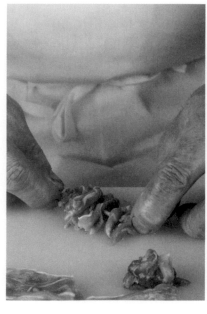

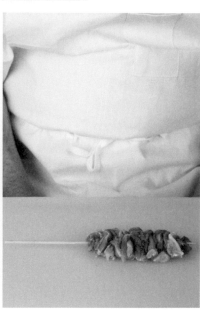

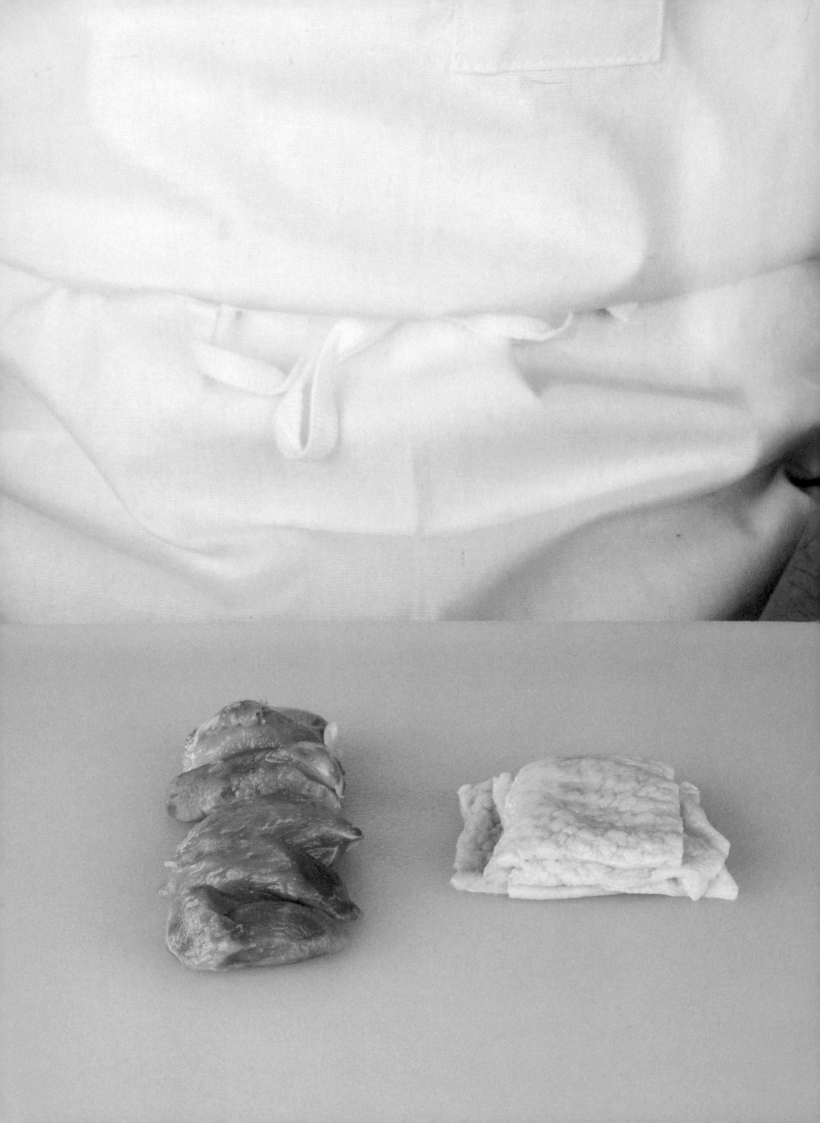

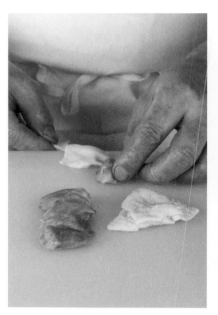
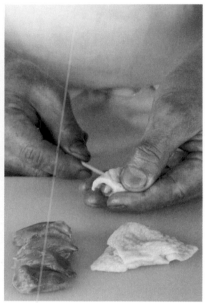
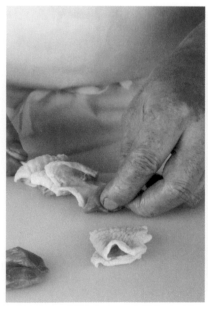
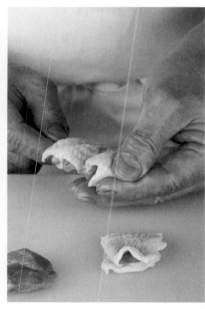
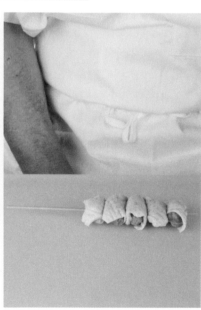

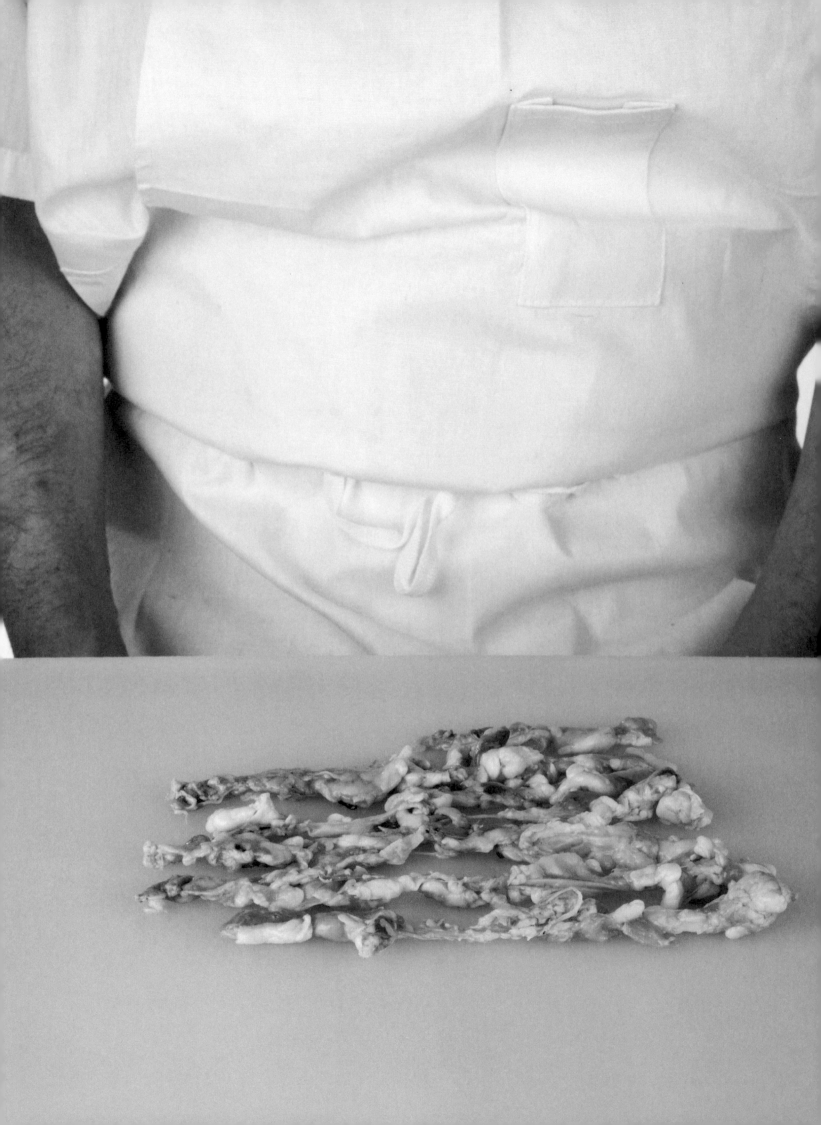

Butchering, a craft older than writing. Yet few of us know what to do with a whole chicken anymore. Even great chefs often don't see all the potential, or haven't the mind to address certain details of the creature's anatomy. There are bits we sense not to dispose of, and yet don't know how to use. Toshi, like all yakitori masters, has developed a system for allocating the entire bird for its appropriate culinary purpose. Saved is each sweetbread from a chicken, and after a day of butchering he might have one skewer. In yakitori, the chicken skin should be made into a translucent sheet. Each ingredient, whether a coffee bean or porterhouse, has a certain inherent character that requires a method. Understanding takes place. Once you have a chicken breast properly divided, it is difficult to go back to eating one that's served as it is just about anywhere. The good news is that these are skills we can all learn and reward ourselves with.

BUTCH-
ERING

a.1—Removing the Head

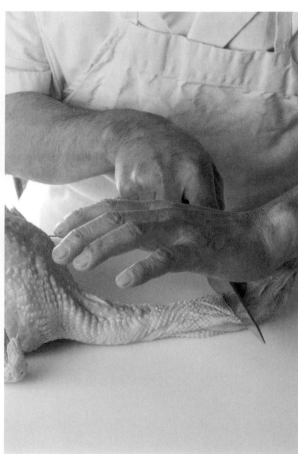

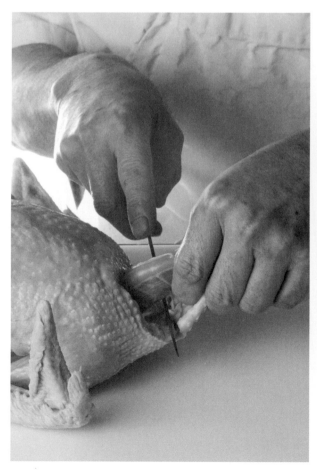

a.2—Removing the Leg

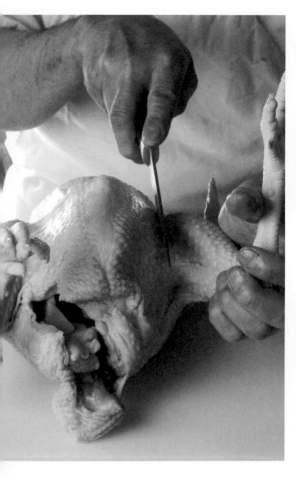
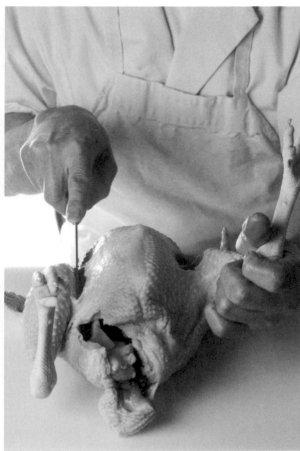

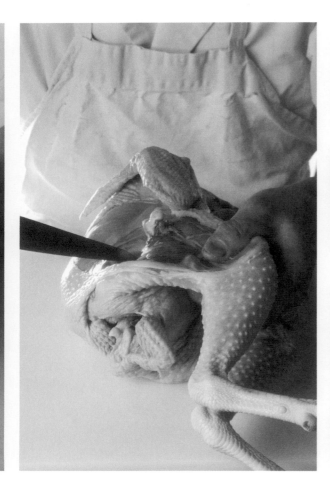

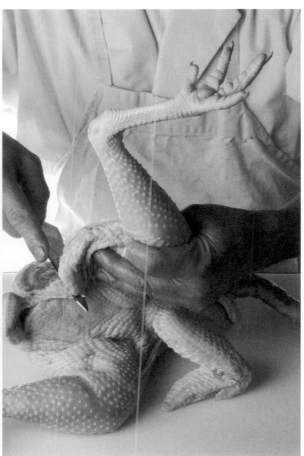

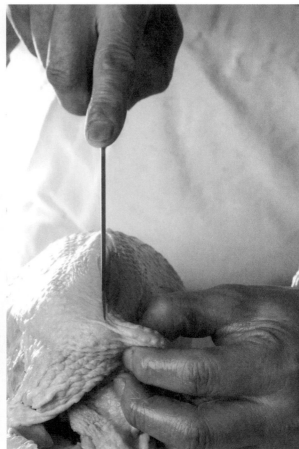

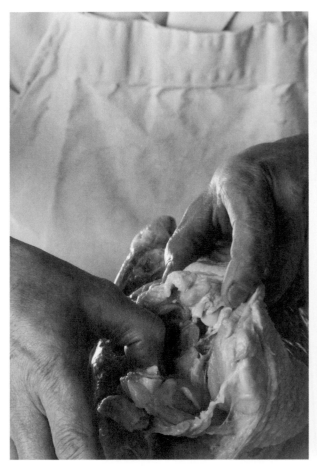
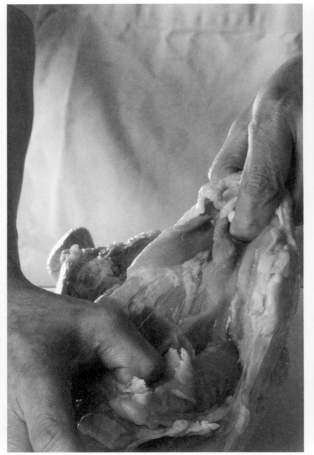

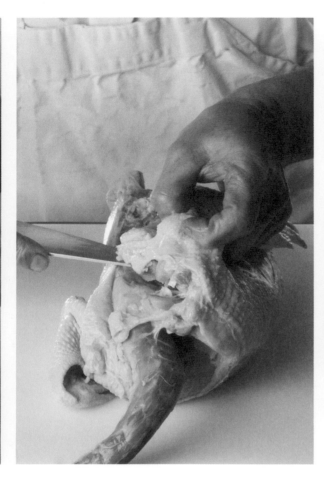

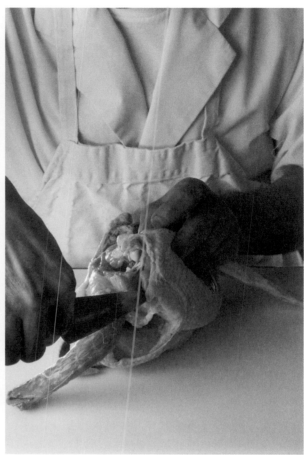

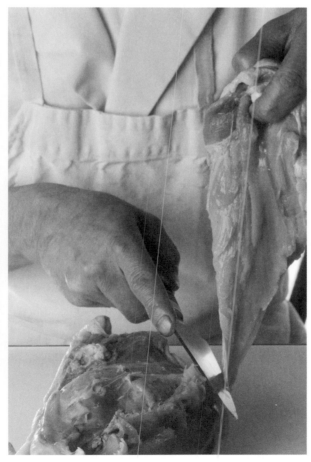

a.4—Removing Premium Breast

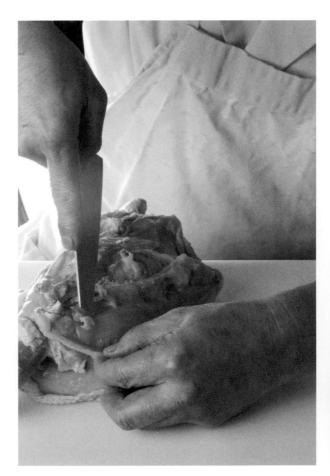

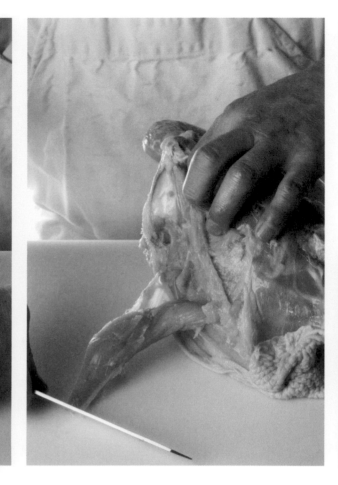

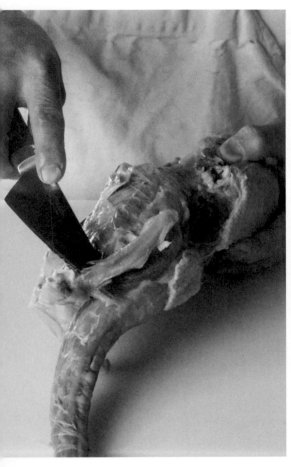

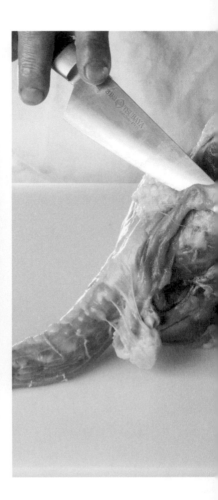

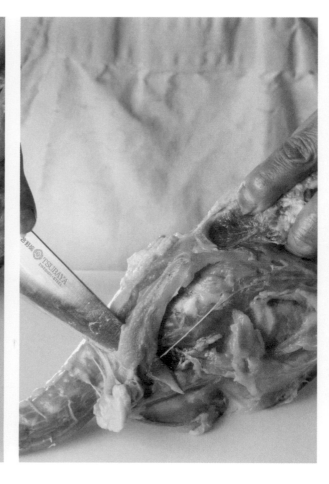

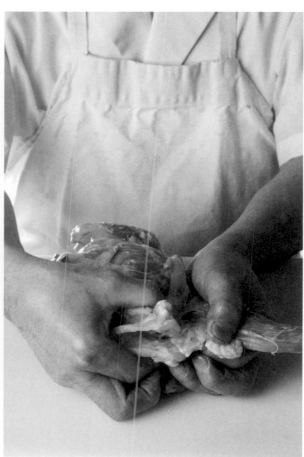

a.6—Removing Sweetbread

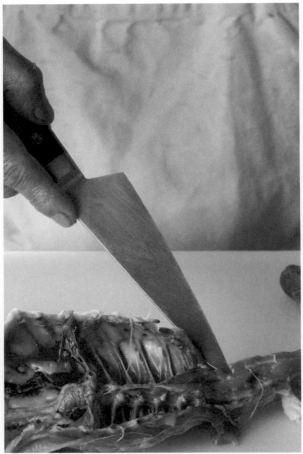

a.7—Removing the Wing and Part of Breast

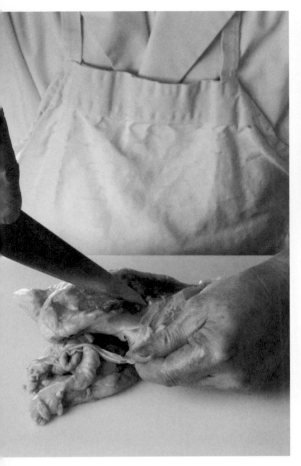 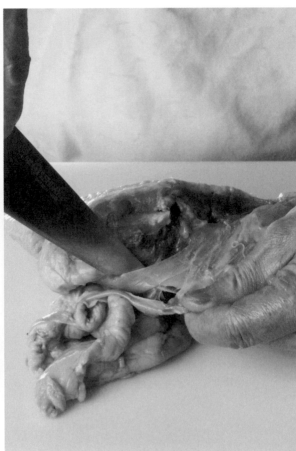 

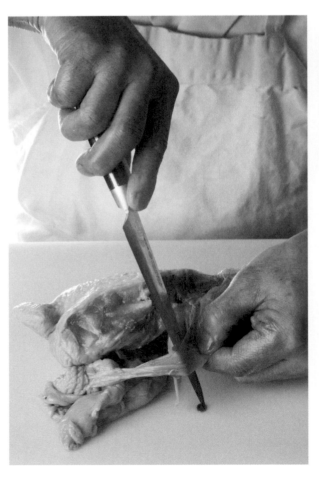 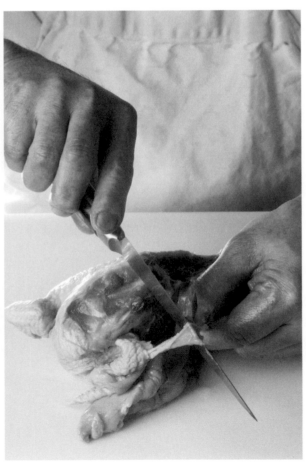

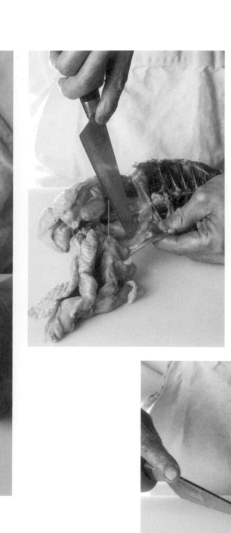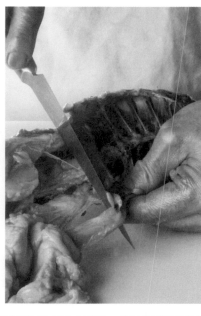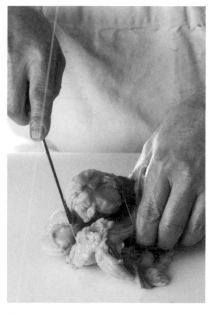

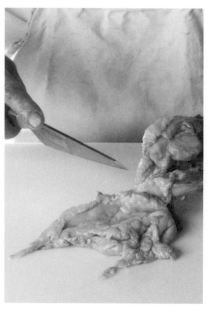

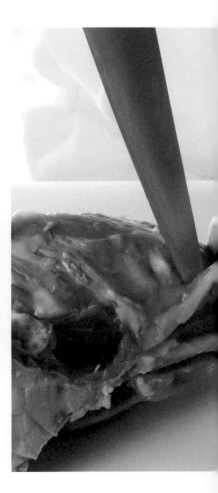

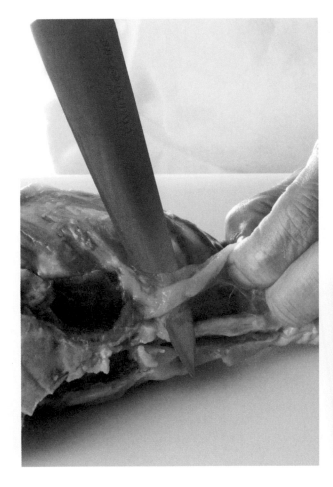
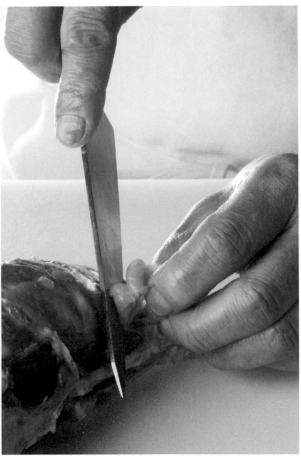

a.8—Butchering Neck

b.1—Rib Butchering

b.2—Removing Wing from the Breast

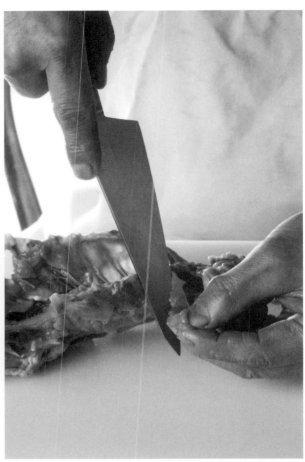

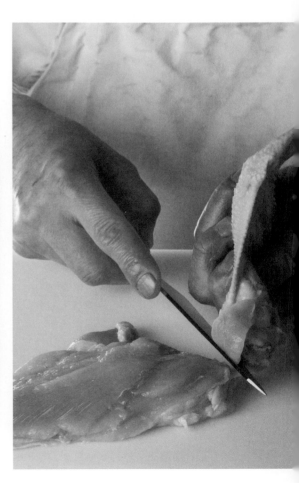

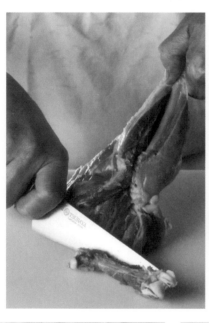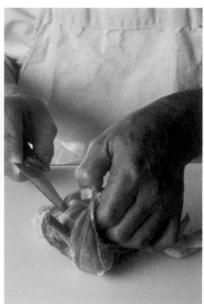

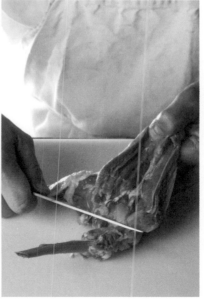

b.3b—Thigh Butchering: Removing Feet

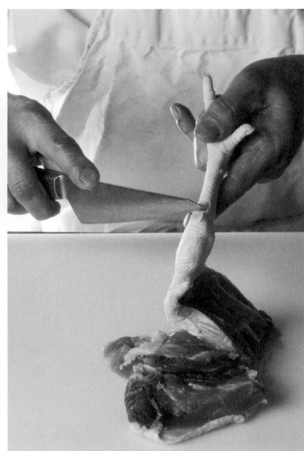

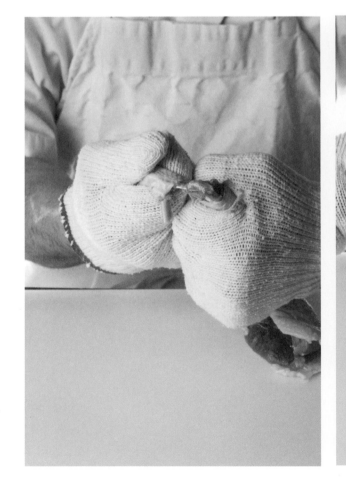

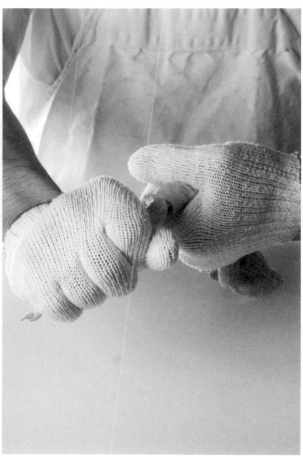

b.3c—Thigh Butchering: Removing Leg and Separating Thigh

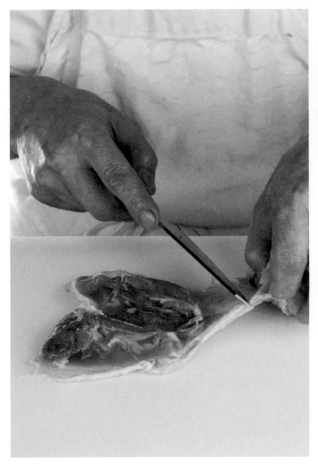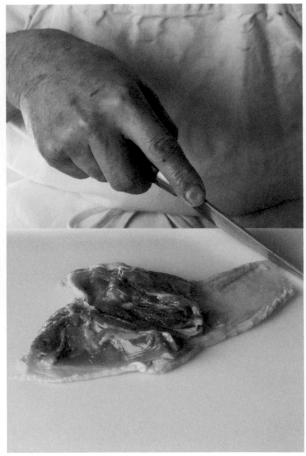

b.3d—Thigh Butchering: Getting Oyster

b.3e—Thigh Butchering: Removing Skin from Thigh

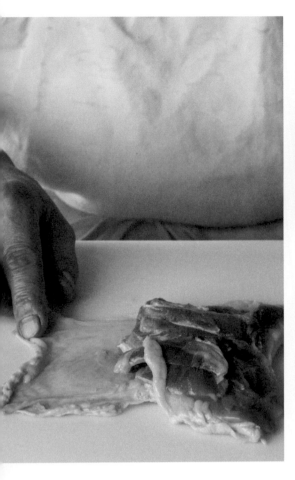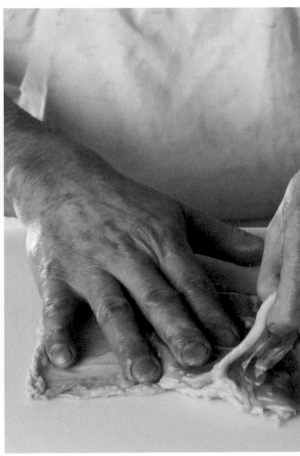

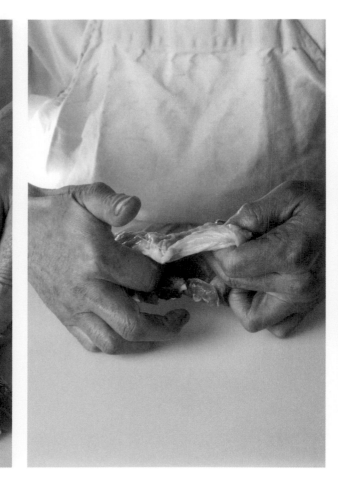

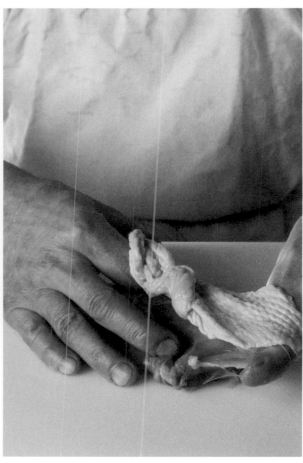

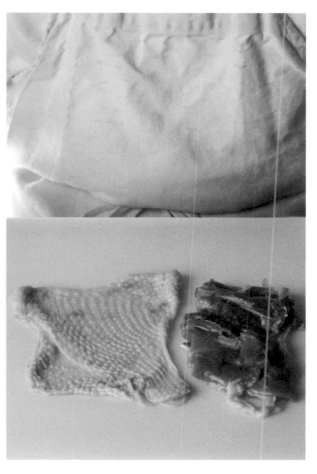

b.3f—Thigh Butchering: Preparing for Skewering (First Piece)

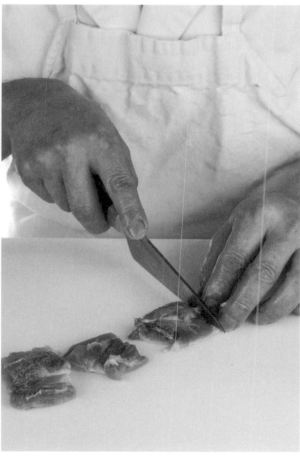

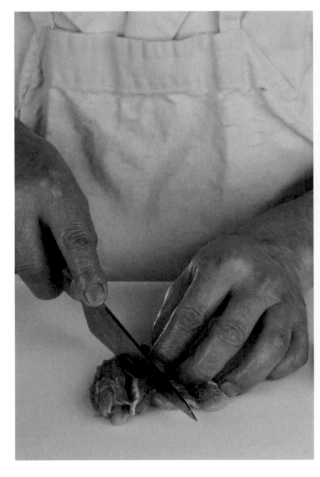
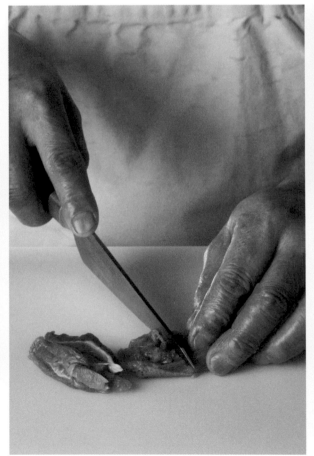

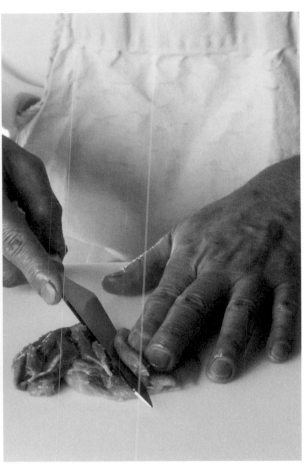

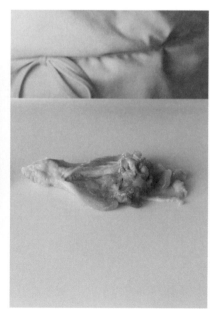

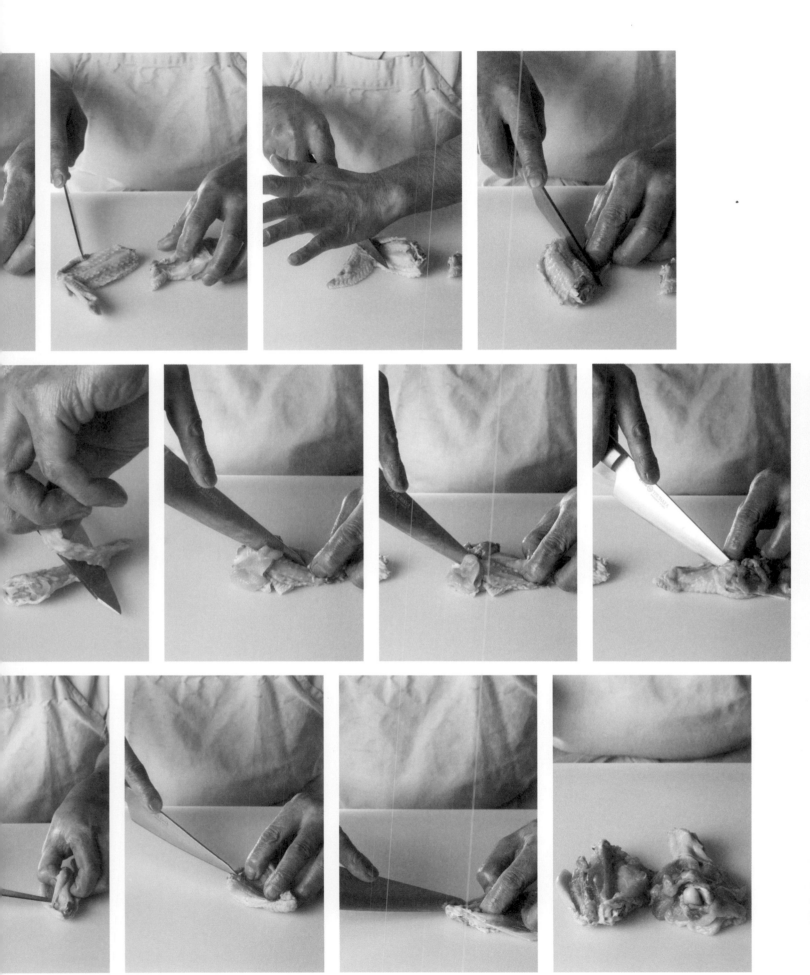

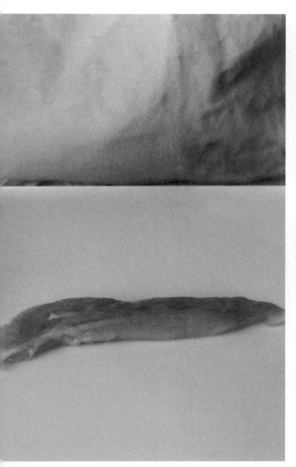

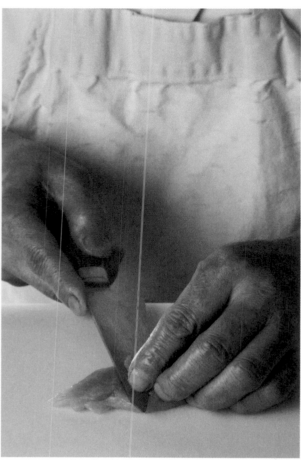

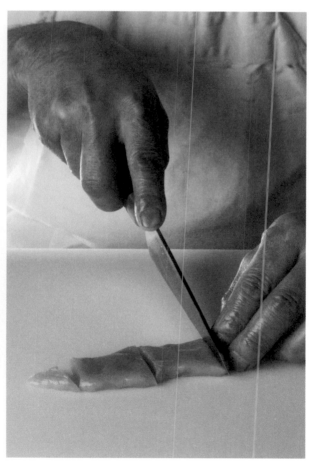

b.5—Breast Butchering (Breast)

 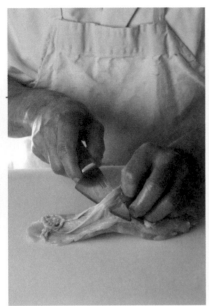 

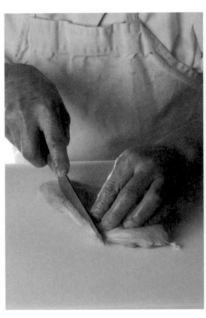 

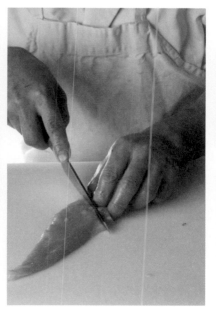

b.6—Chestbone Butchering

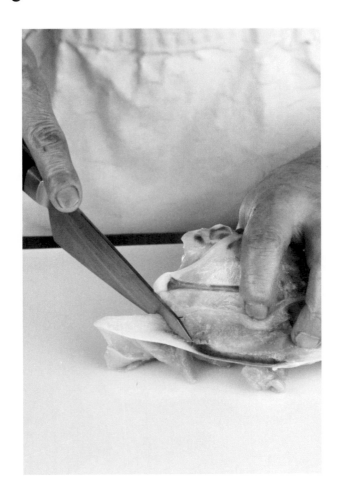

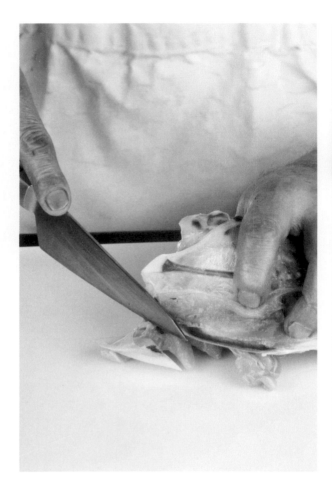 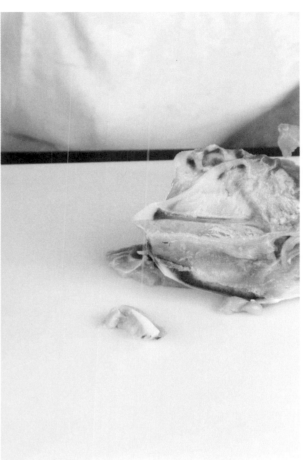

b.7—Tail Butchering

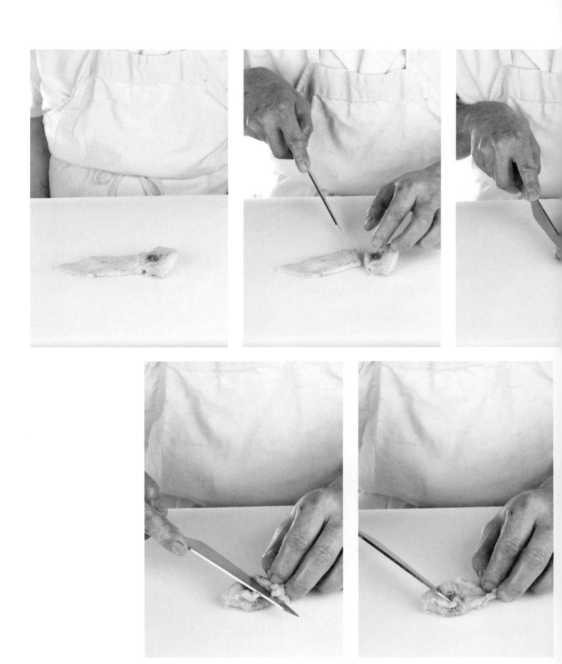

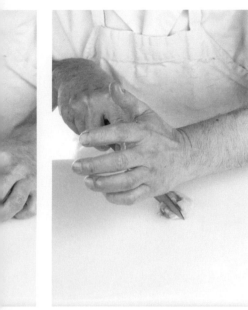

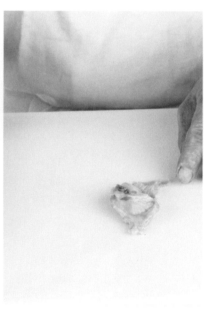

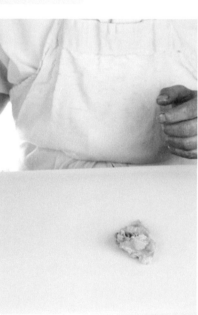

b.8—Skin Butchering

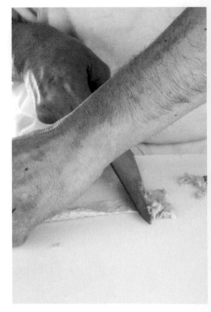

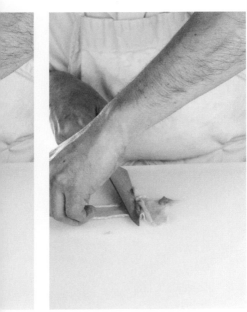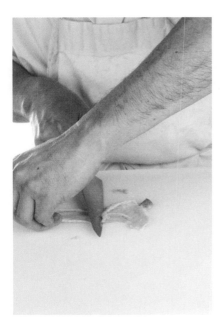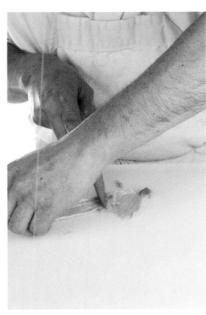

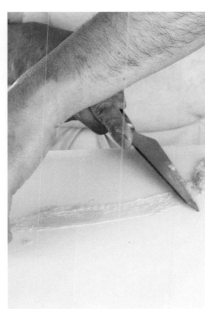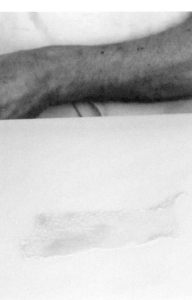

Passion about grilling unites many, and it is my hope that this book proves useful to those thinking outside of yakitori. Not only through charcoal technique, but this detailed, insightful approach to butchering and skewering chicken could substantially affect how anyone barbecue-obsessed (from Texas to Kansas, or even Brazil and Istanbul) prepares. For example, just about all those grilling outside of yakitori treat the chicken breast as a single entity. It took yakitori chefs to break down the breast into multiple parts, for different purposes. So that by the time you've made a chicken breast skewer, it is only a small section of what you consider to be the breast. And the result could be a grilled piece of meat unlike any you've ever tasted.

RECIPES

Burdock Chicken Curry Stew

2 chicken thighs, butterflied then julienned
1 tsp. sesame oil
1 tbsp. Yakitori Sauce (see recipe)
1 burdock
1/2 tsp. curry powder
1 tsp. sweet soy sauce (see recipe)
diced scallions for garnish

1. To clean the burdock, Toshi uses steel wool (traditionally a tawashi brush was used) because there is sweetness and nutrition in the skin. Julienne the cleaned burdock.
2. Sauté the chicken in sesame oil on medium-high heat until half-cooked.
3. Add the Yakitori Sauce (see recipe) and continue sautéing uncovered for two more minutes.
4. Add the burdock and sauté for five minutes, until the burdock is soft.
5. Add the curry powder and sweet soy sauce, and remove the pot from the flame.
6. Garnish with diced scallions to taste.

Chicken Breast Chips

1 chicken breast, cut into eight 1.5 to 2.0 inch cubes or pieces
Potato starch for breading
Oil for deep frying

You will be making these one by one.

1. Take one chicken breast piece and dust with potato starch.
2. Lay the piece on a cutting board and cover with plastic wrap.
3. Using the bottom of a sauce pan, lightly pound the chicken. Don't simply flatten in one spot but move the bottom of the pot around. You should develop a feel for this, as if you're making a flat pancake. The piece should end up about 3 inches in diameter, depending on how thick you like your chips.
4. Repeat with the remaining pieces.
5. Fry in 325 degrees for 5 minutes or so, until the chips are crispy and rise to the surface.

Chicken Breast with Green Beans and Corn

1 cup green beans, roll cut
1-inch piece of ginger
pinch of salt
1 medium chicken breast
pinch of black pepper
1/4 cup cooked corn kernels, canned or fresh
1 tbsp. mayonnaise
1/2 tsp. Yakitori Sauce (see recipe)

1. Bring three cups of water to a boil in a pot.
2. Add the green beans and cook through, about five minutes. Drain and reserve the liquid. Return the liquid to the pot.
3. Add the ginger and salt. Bring to just before boiling.
4. Put the chicken breast in the water until cooked through. Be careful not to let the water to boil, and lower the flame if you need to. The duration depends on the size of the breast, but this should take be-tween ten to fifteen minutes. Pierce or cut the meat to guarantee it is done. Remove the chicken from the pot and allow it to cool until you can comfortably touch it.
5. Shred the chicken either with your fingers or use a knife to julienne the breast.
6. Add the green beans and corn to the chicken. Mix well, then add the mayonnaise, salt, black pepper and Yakitori Sauce (see recipe).

Chicken Broth

In all honesty, when the time came to discuss it, I wasn't sure whether the secret to Toshi's broth should be revealed. But he is always generous, in the highest sense. "You freeze them," he said, showing a pile of bones to me. Contrary to what we're often taught, the pure taste of broth often begins in the freezer, rather than under fire.

Three frozen chicken carcasses, plus any miscellaneous chicken bones, about 10 cups total
10 cups of cold water
(Note: It's important is to try and use equal parts frozen bones to water.)
1 cup of vegetable trimmings or onion/celery/carrots
sea salt
1/3 cup sake, heated so the alcohol will have evaporated.

1. Place the frozen chicken parts in a stock pot and cover with the cold water.
2. Bring ingredients to a boil on a high flame, uncovered. Remove all scum that forms. Lower the heat to low-medium and simmer un-covered for six or more hours, adding water as needed. It should not boil. Alternatively, use a slow cooker.
3. Strain the broth. (Note: Reserve some broth if making the White Chicken Broth below.)
4. Add sea salt to taste.
5. Add the sake to the broth. Place the strained chicken broth in the refrigerator.
6. Once chilled, remove all fat from the top of the broth. (This can be used to flavor dishes such as soboro rice or the gyoza, instead of oil.)
7. Before serving, reheat broth on a low flame, to preserve the flavors.

In the beginning, do not add hot water to the chicken in order to save time. Some chefs have recommended this shortcut lately. However, sim-ilar to the preparation of dashi, Toshi feels there's better flavor when we bring the temperature up slowly and cook the chicken from the inside. Also, if using chickens that aren't freshly sourced, you may want to add a slice of ginger in the beginning. The Japanese use it to purify the taste of pork broth, and it will have the same results with a chicken.

Yakitori Broth Variation: White Chicken Broth

1. Take the strained chicken broth from step 3 above. Add it to the pot of bones you already used to make the first chicken broth.
2. Place on medium-high to high heat and cook uncovered for one hour, at a solid boil.
3. Strain the broth again. Add sea salt to taste.
4. Place the strained broth in the refrigerator. (Note: Unlike the regular chicken broth, there is no sake added to this stock.)
5. Once chilled, remove all the fat from the top of the broth.
6. As above, when it is time to serve the broth, reheat it on a low flame.

Chicken broth with Meatball and Vegetables

Toshi uses the chicken broth to make this hearty soup.

Bring the broth to a light boil, add eight 1-inch chicken meatballs (see meatball skewer recipe for the ground chicken) and cook them in the broth for 6–8 minutes, until they float to the surface. Add sliced shiitake and enoki mushrooms to taste and cook for thirty seconds. Remove from broth and garnish with diced scallions and sesame seeds.

Chicken Wing Confit

Although traditionally confit is reserved for waterfowl meats or pork, Toshi's knowledge of all things chicken makes this one delicious adaptation.

Makes 4 servings

8 chicken wings
1 tbsp. sugar
1 tbsp. salt
1 container of vegetable oil, to cover chicken (Note: If you have chicken fat from the broth, use half vegetable oil and half chicken fat)
1/4 cup arugula or similar greens, to serve the confit on
pinch of sansho

Note: You will need an extremely low flame to prepare this dish properly. A flame protector is useful for this purpose. Also, you can place the cooking pot in a much larger pot full of water as well.

1. For two hours, marinade the wings in sugar and salt in a narrow pot, spreading the mixture evenly on the meat.
2. Add enough vegetable oil to the pot so that the chicken wings are completely covered.
3. Turn the flame on extremely low, using a flame protector if you have one. The pot shouldn't get over 212 degrees Fahrenheit. Cook for two hours then bring to room temperature.
4. Heat 1 tbsp. vegetable oil in a teflon or enamel pan. Line the bottom of the pan with confit, and place on a high flame on the stove. Cook the wings until they're a bit crispy, roughly five to seven minutes.
5. To serve: Place arugula on the bottom of the plate, lay the confit, then add a dash of sansho to complete the dish.

Chikuzenni—Simmered Chicken and Root Vegetables

1 cup konyaku, julienned
2 chicken thighs, julienned
1 tsp. sesame oil
1 tbsp. Yakitori Sauce (see recipe)
1/2 cup burdock
1 cup carrot, julienned
4 shiitake mushrooms
1/2 cup cooked edamame, shelled and cut

1. Boil the konyaku in a pot of water for two minutes. Remove and drain for later use. This should always be done when using konyaku.
2. Clean the burdock. Toshi uses steel wool (traditionally a tawashi brush was used) because there is sweetness and nutrition in the skin. Julienne the burdock.
3. Sauté the chicken thighs in sesame oil on medium-high heat for five minutes, until halfway cooked.
4. Add the Yakitori Sauce (see recipe) and the burdock, and continue to sauté for approximately five minutes, until the chicken is nearly cooked through.
5. Add the carrots and konyaku. Cook until the carrots are almost soft.
6. Add the mushrooms and cook until the carrots are soft.
7. Add the edamame and transfer to a serving bowl.

Curry Chop Chae

2 oz. Bean Thread Glass noodle
sesame oil
1 tbsp. ground chicken
Yakitori Sauce (see recipe)
1 tbsp. carrots, julienne
4 oz. Mung bean sprouts
2 tbsp. Nira, cut into 1-inch pieces
1 tbsp. shiitake mushroom
2 oz. enoki mushrooms, cut into 1-inch pieces
1/2 tsp. of curry powder

1. Soak the glass noodle in warm water for 15 minutes or until al dente. Cut the noodles into three-inch pieces.
2. In a sauté pan, heat 1 tsp. of sesame oil on a high flame. Add the chicken and 1 tsp. of Yakitori Sauce (see recipe). Cook through, about three to 5 minutes.
3. Add the carrots and sauté for 1–2 minutes.
4. Add the rest of the ingredients until cooked through, about three to five minutes.
5. In a separate sauté pan, add 1 tsp. of sesame oil on a high flame. Add the noodles and sauté until it looks clear. Add 1 tsp. of Yakitori Sauce (see recipe) and the curry powder. Cook until well mixed, under a minute. Turn off the flame.
6. Add the vegetables and ground chicken from the other pan to the noodles.

Deep Fried Chest Bone

All the gems thrown away because people don't know what to do. The keel or carina runs along the center of the cavity, from the sternum. There is only a precious one per chicken. Chewy and dense, this is a special dish, for as many love it as not.

8–10 chest bones, split in half—if you don't have much chicken, you can freeze them until you have enough to make this special appetizer
3 tbsp. soy sauce
1 tbsp. potato or corn starch
Soybean or Vegetable oil for deep frying

1. Marinade the chest bones in the soy sauce for 5 minutes.
2. Heat oil in a deep fryer to 325 degrees Fahrenheit.
3. Drain the liquid and pat dry. That's necessary, or else it won't be crispy.
4. Add a thin layer of potato starch to the chest bones using your hands.
5. Deep fry for 5–7 minutes. It is done about two minutes after floating to the surface. Cook until the right color and crispiness.

Deep Fried Gizzard with Soy Sauce and Garlic Flavor

Once a staple across the United States, the gizzard is sadly neglected in these times. Most prevalent in the South, where many still consider it a delicacy, nowhere is it appreciated than across much of Asia.

4 gizzards, split in quarters. (If you haven't got 4 gizzards, you may freeze them until you've enough to make this dish. However, the frozen gizzards will be softer than the fresh, after freezing.)
1 clove grated garlic
2 tbsp. soy sauce
2 tsp. sake
1 tbsp. potato starch (corn starch may be substituted)
Soybean oil for deep frying

1. Begin by making the sauce. Combine the garlic, soy sauce, and sake in a mixing bowl.
2. Marinade the gizzards for at least twenty minutes.
3. Heat a frying pan or deep fryer with oil to 325 degrees Fahrenheit.
4. Drain the marinade off the gizzards and pat dry.
5. Add the potato starch to the dry gizzard with your hands. Otherwise, the chicken will not be crispy.
6. Deep fry for 7–10 minutes. It is done about two minutes after floating to the surface. Cook until the right color and crispiness.

Deep Fried Tofu with Shishito Pepper and Eggplant

1 container firm tofu (usually 14 oz.)
potato starch for deep frying
soybean oil for deep frying
10 shishito peppers. Put holes in each pepper using a skewer or knife (or else the peppers will pop when frying)
1 Japanese eggplant, or any small eggplant
1/2 cup dashi (the instant powder is available at Japanese markets)
1/4 cup Yakitori Sauce (see recipe)

1. Press the water out of the tofu for at least thirty minutes. Toshi places the tofu between two heavy cutting boards.
2. Bring a pot of soybean oil to 325 degrees Fahrenheit..
3. Pat dry then cut the tofu into 1-inch cubes.
4. Dust the tofu cubes with the potato starch.
5. Deep fry until the tofu skin is somewhat crispy, roughly 3-4 minutes. The tofu will float to the surface.
6. Return the temperature to 325 degrees Fahrenheit.
7. Deep fry the shishito peppers for one minute. Drain.
8. Score the eggplant skin and deep fry the eggplant for one minute. Drain the eggplant and cut into 1-inch cubes.
9. Meanwhile, combine the dashi and the yakitori sauce and heat in a sauce pan.
10. Lay the peppers and eggplant on top of the tofu.
11. Cover with the yakitori dashi sauce.
    Optional: Grate daikon on top of the entire dish.

Duck Confit with Wine Sauce

Confit: a classical word evoking hunger for those of us who treasure foods cooked long and slow. This is cooking for people who don't live by calorie charts, and accept traditional nutritious foods. Not exactly Japanese, that doesn't keep the technique from having been adopted by keen chefs. Although Toshi-san no longer serves quail, squab, and black chicken, duck remains part of his repertoire, thankfully.

1 uncooked duck leg
1 tbsp. sugar
1 tbsp. salt
1 container of vegetable oil
Wine Sauce
1/2 cup red wine
1/2 cup plum wine
1/4 balsamic vinegar
1/4 cup arugula, or similar greens, to serve the confit

Note: You will need an extremely low flame to prepare this dish properly. A flame protector is useful for this purpose. Alternatively, you can place the cooking pot in a much larger pot full of water.

1. For two hours, marinade the duck leg in sugar and salt in a narrow pot, spreading the mixture evenly on the meat.
2. Add enough vegetable oil to the pot so that the duck leg is completely submerged.
3. Turn the flame on extremely low, using a flame protector if you have one. The pot shouldn't get over 212 degrees Fahrenheit. Be careful about this, as many recipes these days hurry the meat along by suggesting higher heat, which takes away from the unique flavor of a confit. Cook the duck legs for three hours, then bring to room temperature.
4. Heat 1 tbsp. vegetable oil in a teflon or enamel pan. Place the duck in a small pan, and cook with a high flame on the stove. Cook the wings until they're a bit crispy, roughly five to seven minutes.
5. Meanwhile, in a separate pot, reduce the red wine, plum wine, and balsamic vinegar on a high flame until it reduces to about one-third of the original amount. The sauce should be thick.
6. To serve: Place arugula on the bottom of the plate, lay the confit, and add the wine reduction.

Finger Chicken Fillet with Special Dip Sauce

Makes 4 servings
8 chicken thigh fillets, whole
Pinch of salt and pepper
1 tbsp. all-purpose white flour
1 whisked egg
roughly 2 tbsp. panko
Soybean or Vegetable oil for deep frying
Tonkatsu sauce (available at Japanese markets), or any bbq sauce of your liking.

1. Add the salt and pepper to the thigh fillets. Spread the flour evenly on each thigh fillet.
2. Heat a fryer with enough oil to submerge the chicken to about 325 degrees Fahrenheit.
3. Dip the chicken into the egg then bread the meat with a thin layer of panko. Use your hands to make sure that the panko sticks on firmly.
4. Fry the chicken for approximately 5–7 minutes, depending on the size of the fillet. It will be done about one minute after floating to the surface.
5. Drain and serve with a Tonkatsu or bbq sauce.

Gyoza

Dumplings are happiness. While gyoza are usually served with pork, any number of stuffings exist in Japan. Given that this is yakitori, chicken is once again highlighted. Makes 20 chicken gyoza dumplings

12 oz. chicken, minced (Note: It's better to mix half-breast, half-thigh, if you can)
1 cup Nira, a Japanese garlic chive, diced (Note: Alternatively, you can use 1/2 bunch of scallions, but add one small clove of chopped garlic.)
1 cup cabbage, chopped
1 tsp. salt
1–2 oz. Ponzu serving sauce
1 oz. chicken fat (optional), added to the minced chicken
1 tsp. white miso
1/2 tsp. sugar
1/2 tsp. sesame oil
1/2 tsp. ginger, freshly grated
20 gyoza wraps
Vegetable oil for pan-frying

1. Combine the cabbage, nira, and salt in a mixing bowl. Mix well and drain any excess water.
2. Add the minced chicken, white miso, sugar, sesame oil, and ginger to the same mixing bowl. Knead mixture until thoroughly mixed and pasty. This is your stuffing.
3. Lay out one gyoza wrap at a time and stuff.
4. Heat 1 tbsp. of vegetable oil in a teflon or enameled pan.
5. Line the bottom of the pan with gyoza.
6. Once the gyoza begin to brown, add enough cold water to cover the gyoza halfway.
7. Cover with lid and cook on a high flame for 8–10 minutes, until the water has completely evaporated. The gyoza will begin to sizzle. It should be a little bit crispy when done.
8. Serve with ponzu sauce.

Japanese Style Fried Chicken with Soy Sauce and Ginger

Makes 4 servings

1 boneless chicken breast, cut into six to eight pieces. (Note: Any boneless chicken pieces will work.)
1/2 tsp. salt
1 tbsp. ginger, freshly grated
2 tbsp. Yakitori Sauce (see recipe)
1 tbsp. potato starch (you may substitute corn starch)
Soybean or Vegetable oil for deep frying

1. Add salt to the chicken and knead it into the chicken pieces.
2. Mix the ginger and Yakitori Sauce (see recipe), then marinade the chicken pieces for 45 minutes.
3. Heat oil in a pot or deep fryer to 325 degrees Fahrenheit.
4. Add a thin layer of potato starch to the chicken with your hands. Otherwise the chicken will not be crispy.
5. Add chicken to the hot oil and deep fry for approximately 7–10 minutes, depending on the size of the pieces. It's done about two minutes after floating to the surface, and when they are the right color and crispiness.
6. Drain the liquid and pat dry.

Marinated Grilled Chicken with Miso

1 chicken thigh
3 oz. white miso
3 oz. sugar
2 tbsp. sake
1 tbsp. mirin
1 tbsp. soy sauce
1 scallion

1. Cook the sugar and miso in a sauce pan over medium flame, whisking constantly until the sauce is very soft and light.
2. Add the sake, mirin, and soy sauce and continue whisking the ingredients until it comes to a light boil. Remove from heat and cool.
3. Marinade the thigh in the miso sauce, covering it entirely. Leave the chicken soaking for at least 24 hours, but preferably 48–72 hours.
4. Wipe off excess paste. There should only be a thin layer left on the thigh.
5. Grill the thigh. Alternatively, it can be pan fried with a bit of oil, if you're careful not to burn the chicken; that can occur easily because of the sauce.
6. Once cooked, the thigh can be cut evenly and served, topped with slices of scallion.

Marinated Grilled Chicken with Sweet Miso

1 chicken thigh, upper part
1 cup Sweet Miso (see recipe)

1. Leave the chicken thigh uncut.
2. Spread the miso on the meat, and allow to marinade. Leave the chicken soaking for at least 24 hours, but preferably 48–72 hours.
3. Wipe off the excess paste. There should only be a thin layer left on the thigh. (Toshi likes the grilled miso flavor, whereas some yakitori chefs remove all the marinade.)

4. *Grill the thigh. Alternatively, it can be pan fried with a bit of oil, if you're careful not to burn the chicken; that can occur easily because of the sauce.*

5. *Once cooked, the thigh can be cut evenly and served, topped with slices of scallion.*

Mushroom Ravioli

You're probably thinking what in the world is this doing in a yakitori cookbook. The truth is that Italian-inspired cuisine is spectacular in Japan. Once you prepare this ravioli, you will understand why my friend took one bite and said that he could never eat in an Italian restaurant again. Staying true to Yakitoria, the ravioli are served in a truffle chicken broth. Makes 10 large ravioli.

16 oz. white mushrooms: cleaned, washed, sliced
1 small shallot
1 small Japanese turnip, minced (or 1 red radish, minced)
1/4 stick salted butter
roughly 6 oz. whipping cream
1 package gyoza or dumpling wrap
3 oz. chicken broth
1 tbsp. Yakitori Sauce (see recipe)
1 tsp. truffle oil
Celery leaves for garnish
1 tbsp. shiitake mushroom, finely sliced
(Optional: 1 tbsp. cooked duck leg, minced.)

1. *Melt the butter in a medium sauce pan.*
2. *Sauté the onion until clear.*
3. *Add turnip (or radish) and the mushrooms and cook uncovered until the mushroom juice evaporates, roughly twenty minutes.*
4. *(Optional step: If you happen to have 1 tbsp. of duck meat cooked, you can add this now. Toshi's dish has it, but it isn't absolutely necessary.)*
5. *Add enough whipping cream to the pot to spread evenly on all the mushrooms, roughly 6 oz. The precise amount of cream depends on the mushrooms, as some shrink more than others. You do not want it to be soupy.*
6. *Cook on high flame until the whipping cream thickens, approximately ten minutes. Remove from heat.*
7. *Place this mixture in a food processor while warm and pulse until it comes together, but is not mushy. It shouldn't be baby food. Let it cool.*
8. *Lay down one gyoza wrap and add 1 tbsp. of the mushroom stuffing on top. Dab the perimeter of the gyoza with a tiny bit of water.*
9. *Take a second gyoza wrap to cover it. Pinch around the ends, being careful to remove all air from the ravioli.*
10. *Bring a small pot of water to boil with a pinch of salt. Boil ravioli until al dente, about five minutes. Drain well.*
11. *Meanwhile, to make the sauce, bring the chicken broth to a boil in a separate pot. Remove from heat and add 1 tbsp. Yakitori Sauce (see recipe). Add the shiitake mushrooms until cooked, less than a minute.*
12. *Serve the ravioli in the sauce, drizzling with the truffle oil. Garnish with celery leaf and the cooked shiitake mushrooms.*

Ramen

Hearty and simple, Ramen is much more than the cup of instant noodles most people, especially college students, think it is. Across Japan, chefs offer their spin on the soup, with a variety of broths, ingredients, and meats. The only thing uniting the experience is the pleasure ramen lovers have in slurping noodles.

At Yakitoriya, it is all about Toshi-san's spectacular chicken broth with slices of his homemade chashu, made in small batches for those regulars that can't imagine a yakitori meal without ramen.

1/2 lb. chashu (pork butt)
1/2 tsp. salt
pinch of black pepper
1 tbsp. soybean or vegetable oil
3 oz. soy sauce, plus additional soy sauce after the sauce is reduced
2 tsp. sugar
2 cloves garlic, sliced
1 tsp. ginger, freshly grated
3 oz. mirin
3 oz. sake
1 bunch green onion
6 cups chicken broth
18 oz. Ramen noodles, depending on how many noodles preferred
1 tbsp. sesame seeds
2 cups mung bean sprouts, boiled for one minute and drained

Making the Chashu and Soup Base

1. *Tie the chashu or pork butt with butchers twine. Add the salt and pepper.*
2. *Pan fry the chashu in oil until browned on all sides. The center will not be cooked at this point.*
3. *In a narrow soup pot, combine the soy sauce, sugar, garlic, ginger, mirin, and sake. Add the green onion whole to the pot as well. Bring the mixture to a boil. The chashu should be covered by the liquid.*
4. *Once it boils, bring mixture to a medium-low flame and cook for 30 minutes, covered. Remove the chashu and bring it to room temperature. Reserve the reduced sauce you cooked the chashu in, then drain the sauce.*
5. *Add 1.5x soy sauce to the reduced sauce, as this will be your SOUP BASE for the ramen.*
6. *Cut the butchers twine and slice the chashu into even pieces.*

Preparing the Ramen for Serving

1. *Bring the chicken broth to a boil.*
2. *Add 8 oz. of your soup base and bring this to a boil in a large stockpot.*
3. *In a separate large pot, bring 8 cups of water to a boil. Add the fresh ramen noodles and cook until al dente. Drain the noodles.*
4. *Add the noodles to your soup base, then transfer to your serving bowls.*
5. *Add the sliced chashu, boiled bean sprouts (they are boiled for one minute in water). Garnish with green onion and sesame seeds.*

Salad Dressing Recipe

1/4 cup rice vinegar

1/2 tsp. mustard

1 tsp. soy sauce

1/3 tsp. salt

pinch of pepper

1 tsp. sugar

1 tsp. sesame oil

1/2 clove garlic

1 raw egg yolk

1 tsp. mayonnaise

3/4 cup of soybean oil

1 cup carrot, grated

1. Mix the rice vinegar, mustard, salt, pepper, and sugar together with a whisk.
2. Add the soy sauce, sesame oil, garlic, egg yolk, and mayonnaise, then whisk thoroughly.
3. Add the soybean oil, and whisk until thoroughly absorbed.
4. Lastly, add the grated carrots. Mix it well.

Soboro Rice

Makes 4–6 servings

1 lb. chicken breast

1 lb. chicken thigh

1/4 lb. chicken skin or fat

2/3 cup of Yakitori Sauce (see recipe)

Roughly 1 tbsp. nori seaweed, shredded

1 uncooked quail egg, peeled. (To peel the quail egg, use a knife to tap it on the top.)

1 tsp. scallion, julienned

Japanese red pickled ginger, Beni Shoga

1. Chill the chicken, as it is will be easier to grind that way.
2. Use a grinder or very sharp knife to finely dice the chicken.
3. In a frying pan or wok, cook the chicken over medium-high heat. Do not add any oil or spices yet. Using a strong whisk, pound down on the meat continuously for 15–20 minutes, until the meat is cooked through. Be sure to keep the chicken rotating so that it cooks evenly.
4. Add Yakitori Sauce (see recipe) to the chicken, cooking for an additional five minutes.
5. Remove from heat and strain to remove fat and oil.
6. To plate, add a serving of rice in a small bowl. Add the chicken. Cover the top with nori, scallion, and the quail egg.
7. Serve with the red pickled ginger.

Sweet Miso

1 cup white miso

1 cup sugar

2 tsp. mirin

2 tsp. of sake

2 tsp. Yakitori Sauce (see recipe)

1. Combine the white miso and sugar in a sauce pot.
2. Stir over medium-high heat; notice that it gets easier as the mixture heats up.
3. Once very smooth, add mirin, sake, and Yakitori Sauce (see recipe).
4. Lower the flame to medium-low, and continue mixing. Be careful that it doesn't burn, given all the sugar. Bring it to a very light boil, so the sauce pulses gently.
5. After 2 minutes this Sweet Miso sauce is done. Allow it to cool.

Toshi's Pot-Au-Feu

2 cups chicken, ground

1/2 cup onion, diced

1 egg white

1 tsp. potato starch

1/2 tsp. salt

pinch of black pepper

4 cups chicken broth

2-inch piece of kelp, optional (or add 1/4 tsp. of dashi powder)

2 cups daikon, cut into 2-inch segments

(Note: It's also possible to substitute potato)

1 tbsp. Yakitori Sauce (see recipe)

2 sugar snap peas, boiled, for garnish

1. To make the meatballs, whisk together the chicken, onion, egg white, and potato starch until smooth. Add half the salt and the pinch of black pepper.
2. Bring a small pot of water to boil.
3. Use a tea spoon to make small meatballs, and drop them into the boiling water. Cook the meatballs for 5-6 minutes, until cooked thoroughly. They will begin to float. Strain the meatballs well.
4. Meanwhile, in a separate pot, bring the chicken broth and kelp to just before a boil and add the daikon. After five minutes, add the carrots. Simmer until the daikon until cooked through. A skewer should be able to go through the daikon with ease.
5. Add the remaining salt and Yakitori Sauce (see recipe).
6. Add the meatball to the vegetables and mix thoroughly.
7. Garnish with the sugar snap peas and serve.

Yakitori Sauce (or Tori Sauce)

1 cup soy sauce
1 cup mirin
3 tsp. sugar
3 tsp. sake

Combine all ingredients in a sauce pot and cook with very high heat until the alcohol evaporates. Let cool.

(Note: Used on thigh, liver, eggplant, turnip, and zucchini skewers.)

Sweet Yakitori Sauce

1 cup soy sauce
1 cup mirin
9 tsp. sugar
3 tsp. sake

Combine all ingredients in a sauce pot and cook with very high heat until the alcohol evaporates. Let it cool.

(Note: Used on heart and sweetbread skewers.)

Spicy Soy Sauce

1 cup soy sauce
1 tsp. sriracha. (If you like it spicier add more sriracha.)

Combine.

(Note: Used on the spicy neck and spicy thigh skewers.)

Chicken Rice Porridge

Not only for hangovers and upset stomachs, this peasant dish is made with leftover rice and chicken. Variations on this simple porridge are part of traditional home cooking in Japan. While usually prepared in a small nabe pot, you can also use any small iron or enameled kettle.

1 cup Japanese rice, steamed
1 1/2 cups cold chicken broth
Six small pieces of raw chicken or 1 oz. minced chicken
1/2 shitake mushroom
1 tsp. carrot, julienned
1 tsp. green bean, julienned
1 whole egg plus one additional egg yolk, whipped slightly
1/2 tsp. green onion, chopped

1. Add the rice and broth to the pot over a high flame. Mix well and add the chicken, bringing the mixture to a boil. If you use tiny pieces, the chicken will be cooked.
2. Add the mushroom, carrot, and green bean, then boil for 1–2 minutes, until the vegetables are cooked. Turn off the flame.
3. Add the egg to the chicken rice porridge, and mix well.
4. Serve garnished with the green onion.

Flan

Makes 5 servings

To make the Caramel Sauce:

6 teaspoons sugar
1.75 oz. lukewarm water
Heat on the stove, bringing it to a boil until smoky. Half the mixture should be dark brown. Once you reach this point, add the lukewarm water to the pot. Then immediately turn if off. Please be careful that the liquid doesn't explode on you, given the temperature of the syrup. Add the liquid to the five small glasses which you will serve the flan in. Place in the refrigerator at least until it solidifies.

Flan part:

3.5 cups whole milk
6 teaspoons sugar (+ 3 teaspoons of sugar for the whipped cream)
3 whole eggs
4 oz. heavy cream (+ 2.5 oz for the whipped cream)
Heat 2 cups milk to almost boiling.
Stir in 6 teaspoons sugar. Add the remaining 1.5 cups cold milk and stir this into the almost boiled milk.
Remove from heat.
Stir well and add the three whole eggs to the milk and sugar.
Stir mixture the mixture thoroughly.
Add the heavy cream and stir.
Divide this mixture into each of the five cups of caramel sauce, once the caramel is solid. Pour it in slowly so that the caramel remains on the bottom. Cover each cup with aluminum foil.
Steam on the stove, keeping the cups outside the water.
Steam on high heat for 15 minutes. Then lower the heat and continue to steam for another ten minutes. Check to make sure eggs are firm. Once firm, remove from the steamer, Remove the aluminum foil, being careful not to let any steam into the flan. Allow to come to room temperature and place in the refrigerator.

Whipped Cream for Flan Topping

You also need to make a whip cream. Allow enough time for it to become chilled. Heat 2.5 oz. of heavy cream with 3 teaspoons of sugar in a small saucepan. Stir constantly on medium heat until it thickens. Transfer the cream to a bowl and place in the refrigerator. Top each flan cup with whipped cream. SERVE COLD.

NOTE: Toshi doesn't use vanilla in his flan because he uses excellent eggs and wants to highlight their flavor.

Coffee Jelly

Makes 5 servings

1 package unflavored Gelatine (1/4 oz.)
5 cups hot coffee (Toshi uses a French roast and makes it very strong)
5 teaspoons sugar
In a mixing bowl, add the sugar to the coffee. Stir well.
Add the Gelatine and stir it in completely.
Strain the mixture through a fine sieve. Sometimes the Gelatine clumps or bubbles - the straining eliminates that.
Allow to come to room temperature.
Transfer to five serving cups and place in the refrigerator for several hours.

Ice Cream

(Sesame and yuzu variatons)

Step One—Basic Ice Cream Base Recipe

5 egg yolks
5 oz. sugar
16 oz. of whole milk
16 oz. heavy cream

In a mixing bowl, whisk egg yolks and sugar together until well mixed and the color changes from yellow to cream, about ten minutes.
Separately, mix the whole milk and the heavy cream together.
Heat in a saucepan on high and continuously whisk until just before boiling. Turn off the heat.
Add this milk/cream mixture to the already whisked eggs and sugar, whisking it gently.
Return to the saucepan and heat once again on high until just before boiling, whisking continuously (otherwise it will burn).
Turn off heat.
Place the pot in an ice bath, being careful not to allow any water in. At this point you will need to cool this mixture down immediately so it stops cooking.

Sesame Ice Cream

Hand grind 4 oz. of black sesame seeds. Continue until a paste. Toshi does this in a Japanese mortar, a sribachi.

Add this sesame mix to the ice cream base while it is still hot and stir in thoroughly. Otherwise it won't mix in properly.

Add to the ice cream maker and follow your machine's instructions.

Yuzu Ice Cream

Once the ice cream mixture is cool (otherwise the citrus will react with the cream), add 1.75 oz. yuzu juice. This amount is adjustable, depending on how pronounced a yuzu flavor you prefer. (Note:: The juice is available in Japanese markets, even out of season.)

Add the juice with the prepared ice cream base to the ice cream maker and follow your machine's instructions.

(Option: If you have yuzu peel, dice 1 tsp. of it and add it to the mixture. This will add some texture to the ice cream. If it is yuzu season, you can use the peels of six yuzu diced instead of the juice.)

When deciding where to eat in Japan, it is all about your specific taste. Chefs take pride in their limited menus and dedicated kitchens. A soba shop doesn't offer ramen or udon noodles, let alone steak and eggs. There are restaurants specializing in horse meat, everything wasabi, the deadly blowfish, and pretty much any other item or category of cuisine that comes to mind. Each town has specific ways of making dishes, and there's a commitment to preserving that. Customers notice when a recipe is tampered with, or if anything but the freshest ingredients are served. Perhaps it is part of the purity of the culture, the way a rock in a garden is laid out, exactly as nature sculpted it over millions of years. The Japanese know that to offer the best of something, you have to be dedicated to it, and to it alone. You have to allow it to speak for itself. The family who has been making tempura for three hundred years may know how to do it better than a chef out of culinary school who plans on cooking everything. The tempura family understands what oil is best and the temperature needed for each ingredient. In a tempura restaurant in Japan, you can count on being served something freshly prepared by someone who cares deeply about the product, so that you and your progeny will return for the same experience again. And the reason it is this way is that both customers and restaurant owners care. This is what happens when customers have a palate, and nobody is manipulating them.

DES-
SERTS

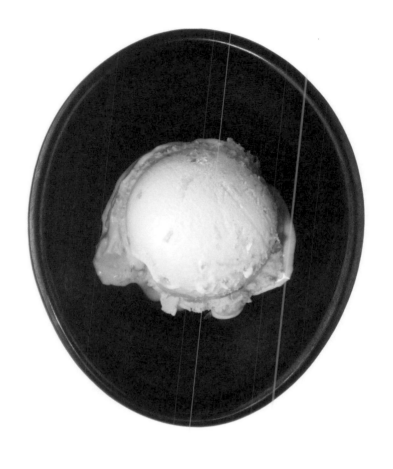

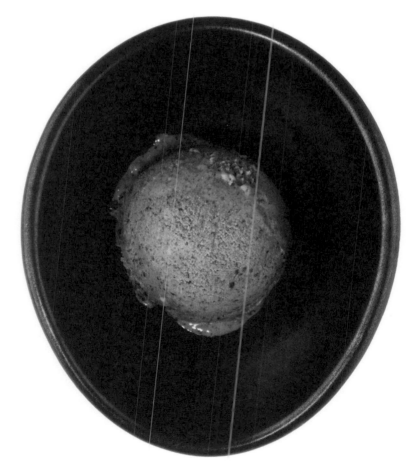

Yuzu Ice Cream—Black Sesame Ice Cream   **159**

INTERVIEW WITH CHEF YUSUKE ISHIKAWA, SHIRO RESTAURANT, SAPPORO

BR: I wonder whether you feel that people appreciate all that goes into yakitori here in Japan.

YI: Many people don't understand the quality, and many see it as simply the grilling of chicken. But here at our restaurant they usually taste our quality is at a different level. I do feel they recognize it, and we have many regulars for that reason.

BR: How did you become interested in yakitori?

YI: I began working here over two decades ago, and I came to appreciate what the previous owner was doing. I wanted to learn everything. Ten years ago I was able to take it over, once I had learned sufficiently.

BR: I assume you love chicken.

YI: Yes, very much so. But also, I have a passion for high-quality pork. The one you order.

BR: I can see why. I wonder whether there is anything about yakitori that you want people to know.

YI: In sushi, the fish is essential. Everything about the quality and freshness. However, in yakitori, the chef's skills are also just as important. That is one big difference. In Japan, the quality of meat and ingredients is high. I was in Italy on a dining vacation last year, and it gave me a true appreciation for what we do here in Japan. I thought the quality would be the same there, but I am learning. Also, the relationship between chef and patron is essential to our cuisine. These are all my guests, here at the counter. It is my honor to bring the best I have to them. I need to do so.

BR: Lastly, what is your favorite skewer?

YI: Katta. The shoulder. We use an Akita Prefecture breed, and I feel the piece has everything. A perfect balance of crispiness from the skin as well as the juiciness of the meat.

BR: I couldn't agree more. Thank you, Yusuke-san, I truly love being able to come to your remarkable restaurant.

ACKNOWLEDGEMENTS

Jon Broida and Sara Motomura-Broida, it is only because of your enthusiasm that I finally went to Yakitoriya. You ignored my pleas about how I don't eat chicken. I'd walked by there thousands of times already, so thank you from the bottom of my heart and stomach for ignoring my resistance and convincing me.

Keno Thomas, at my side through much, with so much heart.

John White, who is as special as his swing.

Dean Briones, to all the special times on the fairways, as well as at Yak.

For Nori Morimoto, a fellow lover of this counter and the one I call at 4:00 p.m. to tee. And Yoshi and Jack.

Julius Smith, fellow Japanophile and whiskey man, you are one of the oh so few I enjoy bumping into at our spots.

Michel Comte and Ayako Yoshida.

Ben Kavian, despite the barrage of questions and analysis, I enjoy your camaraderie.

Naoko and Jason Moore, for the special friendship and all the most wonderful meals.

Michael Mazor, ever the amigo and kind ear. Even for this omnivore.

Toritama's Chef Shiro Izawa and his staff for feeding me so well.

Chef Toshiro Wada of Birdland Ginza, for taking moments with a yakitori-obsessed Quasi-Gaijin like me.

Chef Yusuke Ishikawa of Shiro, for inviting us to your counter before and after you open. Your place is unbelievable. Also, Miho Takahashi of Maruyama Dan, fellow food lover. And Mr. Kitayama, who served us so graciously. Good luck, wherever you are now.

Pabel Delgado, who opened the beauty of Kobe up to me, and for being all-around fantastic.

Margaret Knox, who brings it all together. A special editor anyone would be lucky to know.

Customs Agent Hiko Mizumi, at Narita Airport, for always welcoming me to your country with such kindness and bows.

The Shaheens. Each one.

My uncle Orson, who shared his love of all things gustatory with me at so young an age.

Sima and Baroukh, for the loving support, and for all the grilling over the years.

To Becky, for being there, goofy and all.

To Leila and Aram.

Hichiro Mizutani. With boundless respect. Who else would share a whiskey served with an ice block from Antarctica? Your food is enough to live for, and why I began learning Japanese.

Claire Gerus, who believed in me, and that's huge.

Julia Callahan, a bow for all you give to books.

Alexandra Infante, too. For letting T. join me at work as often as you do.

T. C., without whom none of this could ever happen. This is every bit your book, and my debt to you is forever. Meanwhile, let's get those bodyguards.

To Yoshiko. For every day. The heart. And to your parents and family for the welcome and the slippers.

And, finally, Mika and Toshi, your dedication and care every day, all day, is a marvel. The way you invite me beside the fire makes it possible to live on this side of the Pacific. I hope you feel this book honors all you do.

SOURCES

Japanese Knife Imports

My source for knives of all kinds, and for their maintenance. Classes in sharpening for all levels are available both online and in person, for those inclined. Various pottery and Japanese items are also for sale. A special store and website with all kinds of surprises they will guide you to the right knife for your needs—japaneseknifeimports.com, 8642 Wilshire Blvd, Beverly Hills, CA 90211.

Hitachiya

The sister store to the famous original in Tsukiji, this Torrance, California branch carries all kinds of gorgeous, useful restaurant equipment unavailable elsewhere—hitachiyausa.com, 2509 W Pacific Coast Hwy, Torrance, CA 90505.

Korin

A beautiful store in Manhattan for any manner of Japanese tableware and cutlery—korin.com, 57 Warren St, New York, NY 10007

Toiro Kitchen

The distributor for Nagatani-en clay pots from Iga, Japan, this is the store cookbook author and sommelier Naoko Moore runs. Although not specifically for yakitori, her Donabe are a must for any kitchen, and thus needed mentioning. Food prepared in the various pots is breathtaking. I own a rice cooker, steamer, smoker, and tagine In case of a fire or mudslide, I'd grab them before anything else—toirokitchen.com.

Gion Hararyoukaku

Thirteen generations later, this beautiful storefront in Kyoto sells some of the most revered Shichimi spice blends in all of Japan—hararyoukaku.co.jp, 267 Gionmachi Kitagawa, Higashiyama Ward, Kyoto.